Warship Design Histories

Essex-Class Carriers

ESSEX-CLASS CARRIERS

By Alan Raven

Naval Institute Press
Annapolis, Maryland

Library of Congress Cataloging-in-Publication Data
Raven, Alan.
  Essex-class carriers / by Alan Raven
    p.   cm. — (Warship design histories)
  ISBN 0-87021-021-1
  1. Aircraft carriers—United States.   I. Title.   II. Series:
Raven, Alan. Warship design histories.
V874.3.R38   1988
359.3'255'0973—dc19   88-15590
                                                  CIP

Printed in the United States of America

Contents

Acknowledgments

A number of individuals gave freely of their time and materials, and without their help this volume would be poorer: L. Sowinsky of the Intrepid Sea-Air-Space Museum in New York City; A. D. Baker III of Virginia; N. Friedman of New York; R. Sumrall of Maryland; T. Walkowiak of Pennsylvania; and C. Ratliff of Maryland.

Warship Design Histories

Essex-Class Carriers

Introduction

Of all the vessels that saw combat in the Pacific War, two types contributed more than the others toward victory over the Japanese empire—the aircraft carrier and the submarine. The former neutralized the Japanese surface fleet and protected the amphibious forces that retook the islands, while the latter effectively cut the supply lines from the homeland to the many occupied territories and islands. Both types of ships had seen initial combat in World War I, and World War II saw them achieve maturity and significant effectiveness in action. Of the two, the carrier was by far the more visible; therefore its exploits gained the lion's share of public attention.

Although the thrust of Japanese expansion had been stopped by the prewar carriers during the 1942 battles, it was the war-built *Essex*-class vessels that carried the fight to the enemy from 1944 to the end of the war. Being of prewar design, they were built essentially to treaty restrictions, and although the design was expanded, the desperate need to complete the ships as soon as possible meant that the class was in many ways a compromise.

By war's end in 1945, the vessels were considered to be unsuited for postwar use, being badly overweight, impossibly cramped, and unable to effectively operate large numbers of the new jet aircraft that were soon to enter service, and having reduced resistance to torpedo damage. Their substantial size, however, permitted a continual series of modernizations that allowed effective operation of modern types of aircraft for more than two decades after the war.

Design

The class originated in 1939, when plans were made to build a single vessel to take up the remaining 20,000 tons of construction allowed under the existing naval treaty. Under such a restriction it was inevitable that the design would be based upon that of the newly built and successful *Yorktown* class, also of 20,000 tons displacement.

One of the most important requirements of American aircraft carriers was to carry and operate the maximum number of aircraft over and above any protection requirements or characteristics. The main factor deciding the carrying capacity was ship or hull size, which in turn decided flight deck length and area. Also a factor to be considered was the individual size of aircraft, especially as the newer types were heavier and larger. Flight deck operations could be affected by the number and location of the elevators. Another factor affecting operations was the capacity of back-up facilities such as the amount of aviation gasoline carried and the number and types of spares for aircraft such as engines or wings. These were more important for naval aircraft than for their land-based sisters owing to the higher accident rate inherent in carrier operations.

The need to increase flight deck length and area affected other characteristics, such as the size and layout of the island and the number and disposition of the AA guns of all sizes.

As the design progressed, the new twin 5-inch, .38-caliber mounting was about to become available. In theory, this weapon was to be more effective on a gun-for-gun basis than the existing 5-inch single open mounting as fitted to the *Yorktown* class. If four of the twin mounts were arranged fore and aft of the island, then the four standard side 5-inch mounts as arranged in the *Yorktown* could be dispensed with, leaving a total of four twins at or above flight deck level and four 5-inch singles laid out fore and aft on the port side. This was a 50 percent increase over the *Yorktown*, and the deletion of the starboard 5-inch allowed a substantial increase in flight deck width and area. Close-range AA defense was taken care of by the fitting of the quadruple 1.1-inch machine gun and the single-mounted 0.5-inch machine gun. Fitting four of the former and up to forty of the latter was proposed.

Propulsion underwent a major change from the *Yorktown* class in that the machinery was arranged on an alternating boiler room/engine room basis, as opposed to having all boiler rooms first, followed by all the engine rooms. This new layout gave greatly increased resistance to damage, but demanded an increase in space owing to the greater number of connections needed, and a consequent weight increase.

One aspect of air group operations was the requirement to launch and retrieve over the bow, assuming damage had put the aft part of the flight deck out of action. The necessity then to have a high astern speed threw a strain on the conventional geared turbine machinery. Adoption of a turboelectric drive, however, enabled the ship to maintain a high astern speed. It had a greater weight for a given SHP, but increased economy at a 15-knot cruising speed.

Protection was a subject that caused considerable discussion, and was divided into two main areas. To protect the ship against bombs whether from dive-bombing or high-level attack, a substantial thickness of armor would be required on various decks, with 2.5 inches of armor on the hangar deck to stop a thousand-pound blast bomb, and flight deck armor of 1.5-inch thickness to stop a five-hundred-pound blast bomb.

The cost of armored decks would have been considerable, as added to the ship's displacement was the weight not only of deck armor but also of the extensive structural arrangements needed to support such protection, plus the increased beam necessary to retain the required level of stability, consequent with the fitting of heavy weights high up in the vessel. In addition, and probably most important, would be the mandatory reduction in aircraft able to be carried, up to two thirds of the air group. Such a reduction was unacceptable in view of the offensive tactical doctrine of the U.S. carrier force. The idea of giving a substantial measure of protec-

Table A. *Essex*-Class Designs

	CV 9A	CV 9B	CV 9C	CV 9D	CV 9E	CV 9F	CV 9G
Std Disp't (tons)	26,200	25,300	23,900	23,300	24,250	26,000	27,200
Trial Disp't (tons)	31,270	30,860	29,100	28,700	30,900	32,200	33,400
LWL (ft)	856	836	820	820	820	820	830
Beam (ft)	88	87.5	88	86	88	91	96.3
Draft (trial) (ft)	26	26.4	25.2	25.5	25.9	26.5	26.0
Machinery Type	TE	GT	TE	GT	GT	GT	GT
SHP	170,000	170,000	120,000	120,000	150,000	150,000	150,000
Speed Ahead (kts)	35	35	33	33	34	33	33
Astern (kts)	25	20	25	20	20	20	20
Depth (main deck) (ft)	54.5	53.5	54.5	52.5	53.5	54.0	53.5
Width (mach spaces) (ft)	60	60	58	58	57.5	57.5	57.5
Depth (torp pro) (ft)	14	13.75	15	14	15	16.8	19.4
FD (in)	—	—	—	—	—	—	2.5
HD (in)	—	—	—	—	—	2.5	—
AD (in)	1.5	1.5	1.5	2.5	2.5	1.5	1.5

tion against bombs had considerable appeal, however, and was part of the characteristics of many of the designs that were presented for discussion in December 1939.

The six designs reflected an increase in flight deck area over the *Yorktown*s, a greater number of 5-inch guns, increased protection, and greater SHP to maintain a maximum 33-knot speed on displacements well in excess of the original starting figure of 20,000 tons.

Unfortunately the drawings for designs A, B, F, and G have not been located, but it is believed that the external layout would be similar to those shown.

The navy's General Board decided to adopt design E to be developed further, and as an alternative for further discussion, design F was drawn up with a different armor arrangement, and design G with an armored flight deck but without hangar deck armor.

Design G was rejected (for reasons unknown) and E and F were compared. E gave protection only against shellfire, while F lost some protection against shellfire but had a degree of resistance to bombs. This last feature determined that design F be developed further.

Design F was externally identical to the drawing of design E. Compared to the *Yorktown* class, the island structure is smaller, but the bigger hull and removal of the starboard side 5-inch guns allowed a substantially longer and wider flight deck. The air group was to consist of four squadrons for a total of seventy-four aircraft. It was proposed that the ship carry a fifth squadron composed of eighteen fighters, but as the size of the new types of aircraft coming into service increased, this idea was dropped, as was the number of aircraft carried in a disassembled state to act as spares and replacements for damaged or lost planes.

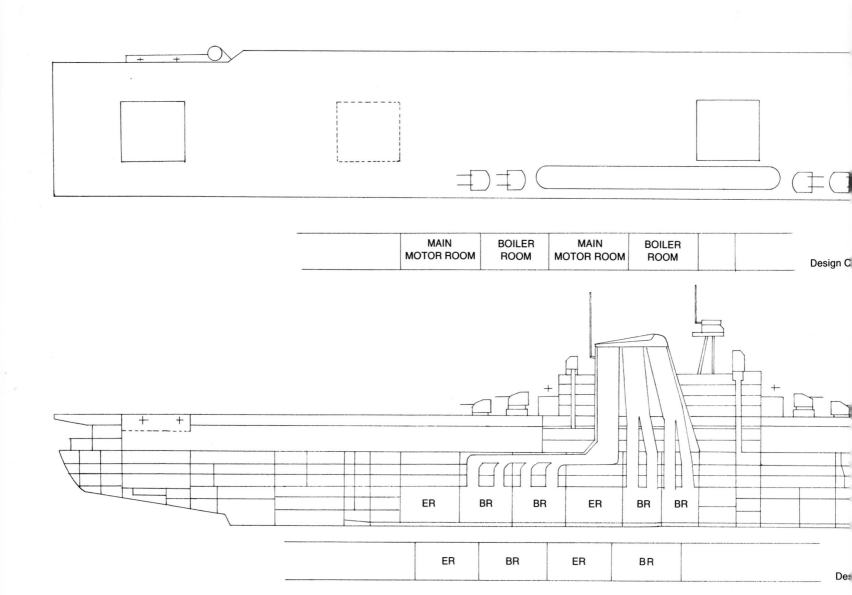

		MAIN MOTOR ROOM	BOILER ROOM	MAIN MOTOR ROOM	BOILER ROOM			Design C

	ER	BR	BR	ER	BR	BR	

	ER	BR	ER	BR			Des

Design CV 9-E, Flight Deck

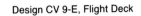

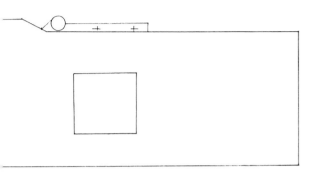

QUAD 40-MM

QUAD 40-MM

ared Drive

Design CV 9-E, Profile

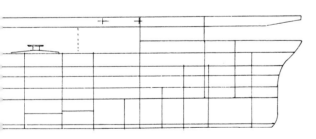

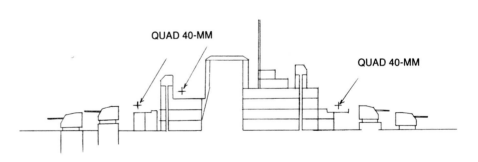

QUAD 40-MM

QUAD 40-MM

CV 9 Design, 23 September 1941

D, Electric Drive

Construction

On 21 February 1940 the secretary of the navy approved the design, to which were added two flight deck catapults and one athwartships catapult forward on the hangar deck.

In May 1940 three extra ships of the CV 9 group were ordered (CVs 10–12). Very shortly thereafter the Congress authorized a 70 percent expansion of the navy, adding seven carriers to the four of the CV 9 class (CVs 13–19). On 15 December 1941, immediately after the Japanese attack on Pearl Harbor, a further two were added (CVs 20–21).

Table B. Ordering Sequence

Ship No.	Date of Order	Contract Date
CV 9	February 1940	3 July 1940
CV 10	May 1940	"
CV11	"	"
CV12	"	9 September 1940
CV 13	August 1940	"
CV 14	"	"
CV 15	"	"
CV 16	"	"
CV 17	"	"
CV 18	"	"
CV 19	"	"
CV 20	December 1941	15 December 1941
CV 21	"	"
CV 31	August 1942	7 August 1942
CV 32	"	23 March 1943
CV 33	"	7 August 1942
CV 34	"	"
CV 35	"	"
CV 36	"	"
CV 37	"	"
CV 38	"	"
CV 39	"	"
CV 40	"	"
CV 45	June 1943	14 June 1943
CV 46	"	"
CV 47	"	"
Total number ordered: 26		

By mid-1941 the ship specifications for close-range AA had changed, with the 1.1-inch mounting to be replaced by quadruple 40-mm, plus four more: two on the island, and one on the bow and stern at forecastle and hangar deck level. The 0.5-inch machine guns were replaced by single 20-mm mountings plus an additional one to give a planned total of forty-four.

Another most important change was decided upon at this time concerning the arrangement of the aircraft elevators. The original design had called for three of these, all laid out just off the centerline of the hull in order to facilitate movement of aircraft in the hangar deck. In very late 1939 the aft elevator was moved from an extreme aft location to one that was about 80 feet aft of the island and so allowed for the storage farther aft of damaged aircraft or those needing maintenance without interfering with the movement of operational planes between the elevators. Another important change to elevator layout was the rearrangement of the midships flight deck elevator to the edge of the flight deck. The prototype deck edge elevator, installed in the carrier *Wasp*, had proved successful.

By December 1942, the *Essex* (CV 9), the lead vessel, was completing. The major change from the mid-1941 AA arrangement was the addition of extensive electronics in the form of air search, surface search, and fire control radars. Actions at the Coral Sea and Midway in 1942 had shown the need for backup radars, and in a ship as large as an *Essex* this was possible. As readied for service in the first weeks of 1943, she was fitted out with two air search radars: the large SK set positioned on the foremast platform, and the smaller backup SC-2 set on an outboard starboard platform at funnel-top level. Surface search was provided for by an SG set at the foretopmast. The backup SG was arranged for at the top of the pole mainmast set at the rear of the stack, but because of a shortage of this particular type of radar, she commissioned without it.

Fire control for the 5-inch weapons was two Mk 37 directors each linked to a Mk 4 radar set, the antenna for these being carried on the top of each director. Control for the 40-mm quadruple mount was by Mk 51 directors positioned close to each mounting.

One vessel of the *Essex* class was commissioned on the last day of 1942 and six during 1943. These were (in order of commissioning) the *Essex*, *Lexington*, *Yorktown*, *Bunker Hill*, *Intrepid*, *Wasp*, and *Hornet*.

At first glance, these early ships appear identical, but a more careful look reveals some differences worthy of note. Affecting launch operations was the omission of the hangar deck catapult from the first two. All seven 'had only a single flight deck catapult positioned on the starboard side.

The *Essex* and *Yorktown* were fitted with eight quadruple 40-mm AA, while the remaining five ships had two more mountings positioned at the after part of the hangar deck on the starboard side, making a total of ten quadruple mounts.

Rig arrangements were split into two main groups in the 1943 vessels: those from Newport News (the *Essex*, *Yorktown*, *Intrepid*, and *Hornet*) had the large SK radar on the foremast platform, while the three from the Bethlehem Yard at Quincy (the *Lexington*, *Bunker Hill*, and *Wasp*) had it positioned on the starboard side of the funnel on an extended outboard platform.

The space left on the foremast platform was taken up shortly after commissioning by the antenna for the new SM height-finder outfit, the prototype of which was fitted to the *Lexington* during her sea trials period, to the *Bunker Hill* in September, and to the *Wasp* in her postcompletion refit in March 1944.

The four Newport News vessels had the backup SC-2 set arranged outboard of the funnel starboard side, while the Quincy ships carried it on the foremast platform aft of the foretopmast. This split suggests that the first batch of SM sets, for which carriers had absolute priority, were sent to Boston rather than to Norfolk.

Every vessel was completed with two Mk 37 directors for 5-inch fire coupled with a Mk 4 radar, and the 40-mm mounts were controlled by Mk 51 directors. The *Lexington* was completed with two Mk 49 directors on the island for controlling two of the four island 40-mm mounts. These Mk 49s were each fitted with an associated Mk 11 radar, the dish antenna for which was strapped onto the side of the director turret.

An essential requirement for air operations was that the ship's aircraft be able to home onto the vessel and her position whenever necessary. This was taken care of by a homing beacon, with the aerial carried at the very top of the foretopmast; a secondary beacon of smaller dimensions was fitted onto several of the 1943-built units on the port side of the funnel on an outboard platform.

By the end of 1941 there was a total of thirteen ships on order (CVs 9–21). This was followed by ten more in August 1942 (CVs 31–40) and three in June 1943 (CVs 45–47), to make a grand total of twenty-six on order or building. The construction of two of these (CVs 35 and 46) was suspended after the war, making twenty-four completed and placed in service.

Wartime Modifications

As vessels began to complete and come into service in 1944, they reflected new equipment and ideas conceived in 1942 and 1943. Perhaps the most pressing need was to substantially increase the close-range AA fire, especially over the bow and stern. This led to a redesign of the bow shape, making it longer and wider to allow the fitting of two quad 40-mm AA instead of the one already allowed for. At the stern a large sponson was added and, as at the bow, permitted installation of a second quadruple 40-mm mounting. To further improve AA fire, two more quad 40-mm AA were placed at hangar deck level on a port-side sponson where the athwartship catapult would have been. The price for this bow and stern extension to fit extra AA was a shortening of the flight deck by eleven feet forward and seven feet aft.

As air operations grew in complexity and intensity, and communications and sensors grew along with them, internal rearrangements were made. These included a shift of CIC arrangements to the second platform deck, under armor. On the island the flag plot on the flag bridge was of necessity expanded and displaced the 40-mm mount forward of it, leaving only three on the island structure. As the 40-mms increased in number, so did the 20-mm mounts, from forty-four in the *Essex* as built to fifty-seven in the first of the long-bow ships.

The *Hancock* was the first of the long-bow vessels, completing in April 1944 with an enlarged flag bridge, eleven quad 40-mm quadruple mounts, and fifty-seven single 20-mm mounts. Two flight deck catapults were fitted. Long-bow vessels completed in time to serve in the war were CVs 14, 15, 19, 21, 36, 38, and 39.

As the early short-bow units came in for yard refits in 1944, they, as with the completing long-bow ships, received the growing number of modifications that operations demanded. Beginning with the *Intrepid* in March 1944, an additional three quad 40-mm AA mountings were fitted on the starboard side below the island at forecastle deck level, two aft on the starboard side at hangar deck level, one at the stern in an enlarged sponson, two at gallery deck level aft on the port side, and with the removal of the hangar deck catapult, two more in this outboard sponson on the port side. This made a total of seventeen quad 40-mm AA eventually carried by most of the original short-bow vessels, and eighteen in the long-bow ships.

Long-range communication in the ships, as built, consisted of a series of long wire antennas strung between lattice towers with the bases at gallery deck level fore and aft along the starboard side. To allow unimpeded flight-deck operations, the towers could be swung from the vertical to lie parallel to the line of the flight deck and at a 90-degree angle to it. By the end of 1944 the aft set of antennas was being replaced by a number of vertical whip antennas. These gave a greater resistance to damage, were of lighter weight, and allowed a greater number of frequencies for transmission and reception.

The greatly increased use of radio channels for ship-to-air communication meant a large increase in the number of shortwave sets. To accommodate these there was a rearrangement of the topmast rig, with the antennas for the extra radio channels radiating from the topmast immediately below the homing beacon, and the SG radar, previously placed on a small round platform, now attached to the side of the foretopmast. Other antennas for short-range ship-to-ship use, or ship-to-air, were attached to the edges of the foremast radar platform, and in many cases from an additional yardarm carried just behind the rear legs of the tripod mast.

As the Japanese began to use radar on a widespread basis, the U.S. countering equipment fell into three categories: intercept equipment, to detect the presence of a radar signal; direction-finding equipment, to ascertain more precisely the signal characteristics such as wavelength and direction; and last, the equipment for transmitting the jamming signals. All this equipment had to have antennas, of course, and locations had to be found for them somewhere on the rig or on the island, with the omnidirectional intercept antennas usually hung from the sides of the funnel on extensions, and the heavier jamming antennas carried on platforms alongside the funnel. The smaller intercept and jamming aerials were fitted from the foretopmast or the foremast platform, or both.

By 1944 the great majority of ships had been fitted with a backup SG set, an arrangement decided upon in mid-1942 but not implemented until much later owing to a shortage. With the second SG set fitted, the rigs of the *Essex* ships became complex and cramped, and suffered badly from funnel exhaust and interference between sets. To overcome these problems, the various antennas were continually moved around, raised, and lowered. By mid-1944 the rig carried five radar sets: two SGs, one SK, one SC-2, and one SM. Despite trying every possible permutation, the interference problem was never overcome.

Newer radars began to appear. The rectangular antenna of the SK set was gradually replaced with the SK-2, which employed a large circular parabolic dish antenna, giving a tighter beam than the SK. The SC-2, with its smaller rectangular aerial, was replaced in several ships beginning in the spring of 1945 by the improved SR set, the antenna for which was similar but could be recognized by its rounded corners and a substantial pedestal. The first ship to receive SK-2 was the *Bennington* in late 1944, and the *Lexington* the first SR in the spring of 1945.

The height-finder SM outfit was replaced on some vessels beginning in late 1944 by the much lighter SP outfit, and in the ships that completed immediately postwar by the SP with the smaller 6-foot antenna.

Fire control for the 40-mm AA mounts was upgraded by removing the Mk 51 director from many vessels and replacing it with the Mk 57 director coupled with the Mk 29 radar, its small dish antenna attached to the lower front of the director. By war's end, the 40-mm AA mounts began to receive the Mk 63 director, similar in appearance to the Mk 51 but used with the Mk 34 radar. In this case the dish antenna was mounted directly on the top of the associated 40-mm AA mount, and not on the director itself.

The number of 20-mm mounts remained the same through 1944, at about fifty-six or fifty-eight guns in single mounts, but as a measure to try to increase AA fire, they began to be replaced in 1945 with twin 20-mm mounts, so that, for example, the *Lexington* after an April 1945 refit carried twenty-five twin guns; in addition she was fitted experimentally with six quadruple 0.5-inch mountings of an army design, as was the *Wasp* (which got only five such mountings).

As the AA weapons and the sensors and communications grew, so did the aircraft carried, in both number and size. An early 1943 complement of four squadrons consisted of thirty-six fighters, thirty-six dive-bombers, and nineteen torpedo bombers, for a total of ninety-one aircraft, plus nine more in a broken-down state as a reserve. By war's end the air group was usually made up of thirty-six fighters (Hellcats), thirty-six fighter bombers (Corsairs), fifteen dive-bombers (Helldivers), and fifteen torpedo bombers (Avengers), for a total of 102 planes.

The later types of aircraft were considerably heavier than the 1943 types. They were bigger and took up more deck space, in most cases carried heavier weapon loads, and consumed more fuel. It would be natural to expect the above factors to reduce the efficiency of the air group as opposed to the earlier period, but the need for more ammunition, bombs, and so on, and for more aviation gasoline was more than accommodated by an efficient fleet train, and launch, retrieval, and deck movements were refined and improved as the war progressed. An example of this was the use of the flight deck catapults; in a number of the early units only one was installed and used for a small percentage of launches, but as the later ships completed with two, and earlier ones were similarly refitted, so did the usage increase; by war's end, carriers of the *Essex* class were launching up to 40 percent of planes by catapult.

The effect of all these additions for the ships and their air groups was to seriously affect habitability. As designed, *Essex*-class carriers were to accommodate a total of 2,386 personnel; however, as built the *Essex* had 3,100 officers and men, and by war's end the *Intrepid* had 382 officers and 3,003 men for a total of 3,385. Others of the class had similar complements.

By 1944, only one year after the first of the class had entered service, every ship was severely overweight, with a consequent reduction in stability, which in turn affected their ability to survive battle damage, especially underwater hits from torpedoes. The *Lexington* and *Intrepid* were torpedoed, but the hits were at the sterns and did not cause anywhere near a serious loss of stability. As designed, the class could take two torpedo hits and still retain enough stability to survive, but by late 1944 this margin had been reduced by 50 percent.

As the Pacific War unfolded, the greatest danger turned out to be from bombs and bomb-laden suicide planes, with most of the actual damage caused by aviation gasoline weapon loads and torpedo explosions, and subsequent large-scale fires. In only a very few cases was the ship in any danger of sinking.

The most notable example was probably that of the *Franklin*, which took bomb hits in March 1945 that ignited fuel, rockets, and loaded-up aircraft. The danger of sinking was in fact due to enormous amounts of water played into the fire at the hangar deck level, the actual damage being kept from going to the lower decks in any real measure. To reduce the effect on stability of large amounts of water used for fire fighting, the ships were very often partially flooded to ensure a list of five to seven degrees to allow a rapid runoff of water from the hangar through the side roller doors and over the side. Many photos are incorrectly captioned as showing ships burning and listing from damage, when, in fact, the visible list was purposely imposed.

After evaluating the performance of the *Essex*-class carriers in the 1943–45 period, there can be no doubt that they were the most effective of all the carrier classes and types of any nation, and were also the most efficiently operated. They were able to operate enough strike aircraft to produce substantial damage to large enemy surface units, and when these were combined with the complement of fighter bombers carried in the last year of operations, the effect on shipping was devastating. Where the carriers perhaps lacked a really effective punch was in attacking large land targets, such as those on the Japanese mainland. In such cases, the attack planes lacked the weight of bombs needed to produce real damage on a blanket basis, and also had to be prepared to defend themselves from very large numbers of land-based planes. In these situations the offensive nature of carrier warfare changed to a defensive one. Thus, the carriers' very effectiveness as an offense in the open ocean, against shipping, and in coverage for island invasions brought them eventually to face large-scale land-based attacks, a situation for which no carrier is really designed or prepared.

Because the carriers were designed initially to meet a 20,000-ton treaty limit, it is difficult to lay much criticism upon them. Every design regardless of any lack of restriction is a compromise. When there is a fixed limit upon displacement, the compromises or balance between such features as cost, size, numbers, or operating doctrine become more difficult to resolve. It can be argued that *Essex*-class vessels were open to bomb attack: the flight deck was completely without protection, thereby allowing bombs to penetrate and explode in the hangar with devasting results, and this in fact happened on many occasions. Against this must be balanced the large reduction in air group strength if an armored flight deck had been fitted.

One feature of construction that can be the subject of valid complaint was the part of the ventilation system that supplied air to the second and lower decks. All the ships completed during the war were supplied by a vent system with aft-situated intakes. The fresh air was fed at second-deck level inside the ship along the port side for two-thirds of its length. Along the passage were various openings to carry the fresh air to compartments and lower decks. The arrangement allowed smoke and fumes from battle damage to permeate the various compartments and lower decks via the long passage. This flaw in design was brought home in the 1944 and 1945 attacks. Ships having repairs and refits beginning in the first months of 1945 saw the blocking off of the long horizontal vent trunk at the second deck, with the air provided instead by making a number of additional intakes along the port side.

The Postwar Years

With the end of the Pacific War in August 1945, the carriers on station were retained until occupation and stability of the Japanese islands had been achieved and then engaged in Operation Magic Carpet—bringing home the many thousands of U.S. soldiers.

Of the twenty-six vessels ordered, the *Reprisal* and *Iwo Jima* were canceled in the last days of the war while still incomplete, and the *Leyte, Kearsarge, Princeton, Valley Forge,* and *Philippine Sea* completed in the postwar months, while the *Oriskany* was suspended and eventually completed in 1950 to a revised design.

As Operation Magic Carpet wound down, the war-built *Essex*es were laid up in reserve, most of them in 1947. Those kept operational received minor refits mainly connected with radar and communications, with the *Boxer, Leyte, Antietam, Princeton, Valley Forge, Philippine Sea,* and *Kearsarge* each having their SK or SK-2 sets removed and replaced with SX. This set combined the long-range air search requirement with height-finder needs, and therefore the SM or SP set was also dispensed with. Other modifications included a slightly lower number of aircraft carried, and the omission on those postwar-built ships of the three starboard outboard 40-mm quadruple AA mounts by the island. (These

were removed from the earlier-built vessels not immediately destined for reserve.)

The fleet of *Essex*es was gradually reduced to reserve status through the 1946–50 period, so that upon the outbreak of the Korean War in June 1950 only four were on active duty: the *Valley Forge, Philippine Sea, Boxer,* and *Leyte.* They were immediately sent to Korea for duty there, and were joined in the autumn of 1950 by the recommissioned *Princeton,* and in 1951 by the *Bon Homme Richard* and *Antietam.* The last three served in very much their late World War II configuration and equipment. The seven unmodernized vessels were joined during the 1951–53 period by four newly modernized ones— the *Essex, Kearsarge, Oriskany,* and *Lake Champlain*—making a total of eleven that served off Korea.

The greatest factor that affected carrier design, usage, and modernization in the early postwar years was the introduction of the jet aircraft with all its differences. Jets were heavier and bigger, therefore imposing smaller air groups. They required a much higher takeoff speed, and the available flight deck was too short to allow a rolling takeoff; thus all jets would have to use catapults, which would have to be of increased power to safely fly off the jets at their higher speeds. Heavier weights and larger size meant stronger decks and bigger elevators. Jets initially flew on aviation gasoline, but it was too volatile; a solution was found in a blend of gasoline and high-energy aircraft fuel, but this process of blending had to be performed on board. Fuel consumption was considerably higher than for piston-engine planes.

In addition to the new generation of aircraft, weapon loads had changed, with a variety of streamlined bombs being used, and these demanded a greater volume of magazine space per ton of load.

Sensors and communications advanced, and a new family of radars was developed, including navigational radars and those for blind approach and carrier-controlled approach (CCA). Such was the revolution in electronics and its proliferation that the original tripod mast was unable to accommodate the new equipment.

All the new requirements could not be met even by a refit; what was needed was a major modernization. Eight *Essex* ships were put in hand for modernization, known as SCB-27A, beginning in the latter part of 1948. The *Oriskany* had had construction suspended at the end of the war; she completed to SCB-27A in September 1950.

SCB-27A modernizations had the following features:

- Removal of the four twin 5-inch mounts.
- A reduced and streamlined island with a greatly heightened funnel structure.
- Removal of the tripod foremast and radars thereon and installation of a heavy pole mast.
- Removal of 40-mm and replacement by twin 3-inch automatic mountings.
- Removal of all 20-mm mounts.
- Removal of Mk 12/22 fire control radars from the Mk 37 directors and replacement by Mk 25 radar.
- Strengthened flight deck in way of landing area.
- Removal of H4 catapults and replacement with H8 catapults.
- Increased stowage for aviation gasoline.
- Increased plane refueling capacity.
- Blistered hull to retain buoyancy lost due to increased topweight.
- Installation of new radars for air search, height finder, surface search, and aircraft marshaling functions.
- Installation of larger flight deck centerline elevators.
- Removal of side armor along the waterline.

SCB-27A modernization was followed beginning in 1951 with six vessels given the SCB-27C modernization. SCB-27C differed in several aspects, the four most important being:

- Angled deck.
- Steam catapults (C11 type).
- Provision for nuclear bomb assembly.
- Removal of the aft flight deck elevator and addition of a second deck-edge elevator fitted starboard side aft.

The SCB-27C conversions were split into two groups of three. The *Intrepid, Ticonderoga,* and *Hancock* were the first three to receive SCB-27C and were just too early to be fitted with the new angled deck, but did receive the other features listed above.

The second group of three ships—the *Lexington, Bon Homme Richard,* and *Shangri-La*—were fitted with the angled deck. It can be argued that the angled deck, along with the jet airplane and the steam catapult, had a greater effect upon carrier efficiency than any other advancement in that it allowed landings to be other than a "land or crash" operation. If the aircraft missed the arrester wires, it had enough power to take off over the angled part of the deck without the possibility of being brought to a forcible halt by the crash barrier or, worse, of bouncing over the barrier and into any aircraft parked at the fore end of the flight deck.

The first angled deck was a painted-on angle on a British light carrier in 1951. This proved to be a successful arrangement, and a similarly successful experiment was performed on the American carrier *Midway* shortly thereafter.

The first true angled deck, one in which the deck gradually extended outboard at an angle, was built onto the *Antietam* in December 1952. This ship was subsequently used for training.

To further modernize the *Essex* class, program SCB-125 was initiated, which gave an angled deck, a fully enclosed "hurricane" bow to improve seaworthiness, improved arrester gear (Mk 7), and an increase in area of the forward elevator to 70 feet. Large areas of the flight deck were given metal covering. Of the nine ships that had received SCB-27A modernizations in the early fifties, one, the *Lake Champlain*, was not brought up to SCB-125 standard but served in 27A configuration until decommissioned in 1966. She never returned to service. The *Oriskany* was given an SCB-125A modernization, which was in effect a full 27C modernization. The remaining seven ships—the *Essex, Yorktown, Hornet, Randolph, Wasp, Bennington,* and *Kearsarge*—were converted to SCB-125.

The first three ships of the 27C program that retained the axial or nonangled deck were later upgraded to the full SCB-27C configuration and fit.

The modernization programs left four vessels completely unchanged. These were the *Antietam* (used solely for training until withdrawn from service in May 1963) and the *Boxer, Princeton,* and *Valley Forge*, which were converted into helicopter assault carriers (LPHs) in 1959 for the first two and in 1961 for the third.

By the early 1960s the class composition was:

• *Franklin* *Bunker Hill*	Decommissioned immediately in 1945 and never returned to service
• *Leyte* *Tarawa* *Philippine Sea*	Served unmodernized
• *Antietam*	Fitted with prototype angled deck but not modernized
• *Boxer* *Princeton* *Valley Forge*	Remained unmodernized but converted to become helicopter assault ships
• *Lake Champlain*	Modernized to SCB-27A (without an angled deck)
• *Essex* *Yorktown* *Intrepid* *Hornet* *Ticonderoga* *Randolph* *Lexington* *Wasp* *Hancock* *Bennington* *Bon Homme Richard* *Kearsarge* *Oriskany* *Shangri-La*	All with full modernizations (angled deck, enclosed bow, etc.)

As the war in Vietnam increased in intensity from the mid-1960s, so did the support given by the converted ships of the *Essex* class. Although they carried up-to-date sensors and communications, size was against them: only two catapults as against four in the new ships, a much smaller air group, and the inability to carry the high-performance Phantom aircraft. To enable them to perform at a reasonably acceptable level of efficiency, they received a series of upgrades, and this brought them to the limit that their age and size would allow. No more could be done, and despite regular care and maintenance, they were wearing out.

With the end of the Vietnam War, the need for large numbers of carriers ceased, and by 1976 all had been withdrawn from active service. The *Lexington* was kept active as a training carrier and at the time of writing is still employed as such. The *Intrepid* and *Yorktown* remain as museum ships, and the *Bennington, Bon Homme Richard, Oriskany,* and *Hornet* are laid up in reserve. The *Shangri-La* is hulked in poor condition at Philadelphia awaiting disposal for scrapping or for use as a museum ship.

Particulars

LOA (short-hull vessels)	872'0"
LOA (long-hull vessels)	888'5"
LWL	820'0"
Beam (at waterline)	93'0"
Width (extreme)	147'6"
Draft (at full load)	30'10"
SHP (designed)	150,000
SHP	154,000
Speed (designed)	33 knots
Speed at 34,000 tons	33 knots
Size of flight deck (long-hull vessels)	862' × 108'
Size of flight deck (short-hull vessels)	846' × 108'
Design displacement	33,400 tons
Design standard displacement	27,500 tons
Design full load	36,380 tons
Boilers	8
Diesel generator capacity	2,250 KW
Endurance (at 15 knots, designed)	20,000 NM

Armament (as completed) for the *Essex*
  12 5" guns on 4 twin mounts and 4
    single mounts
  32 40-mm guns on 8 quadruple Mk 4
    mountings
  44 20-mm Oerlikon guns on 44 single
    mountings

Protection

Hangar deck	1.5"
4th deck	1.5"
Side belt	4"–2.5"
Steering gear compartment (sides)	4" class B armor
Steering gear compartment (top)	2.5"

Wartime Photographs

The Lexington, an early unit of the *Essex* class, at launch. The picture shows the many openings to the hangar side. (Official U.S. Navy photograph)

A bow view of the *Essex* being towed to the fitting-out pier after launch.
(Official U.S. Navy photograph)

The *Essex*, the lead ship of the class, on her commissioning day, 31 December 1942, departing her builder, Newport News Ship Building and Dry Dock, en route to Norfolk Navy Yard.

It is always necessary to ascertain the stability range of a class of ships at the earliest possible date. The *Essex* was therefore inclined at the builder's yard in an almost finished state in December 1942. The on-board picture shows that she lacks the SK and SC air search radars and the Mk 4 fire-control radars. The Mk 4s were fitted by the end of the month, but the air search sets were installed in Norfolk Navy Yard after she left the builder's.

As built, the early units lacked large numbers of 40-mm quadruple
mounts, but not the 20-mm mounts, as this picture of the *Yorktown* taken
in April 1943 shows. She is seen here undergoing sea trials, and displays
the initial rig configuration in which the outboard SC radar is carried
low down to starboard of the funnel. This position adversely affected the
radar's performance, and the first modifications that the early Newport
News units received was the raising of the antenna by several feet. (Official U.S. Navy photograph)

A quarter view of the *Intrepid* leaving Norfolk Navy Yard in late November 1943, following a refit carried out after completion. In this refit the rig was changed in that the SM height-finder radar was installed on the foremast. This in turn displaced the SC, which was then fitted on the top of a pole mast on the port side of the funnel. Two single 20-mm guns were added to one of the starboard side bridge platforms at this time.

A close-up rear view of the *Hornet* soon after completion, seen here leaving Norfolk Navy Yard. The *Hornet* was one of the first carriers to receive dazzle-style camouflage.

This picture of the *Hornet* shows bomb transfers taking place at sea and
was taken while she was operating off Iwo Jima in February 1945, showing the effect of sustained operations on her weathered paintwork.

Landing is never easy, regardless of weather; here the landing officer has stepped out from behind the protective wind screen, perhaps to give extra emphasis to his directions. Taken on board the *Intrepid* in 1944.

The *Essex* class was designed to be able to launch aircraft over the stern and retrieve over the bow. Although later-built units were completed without arrester wires at the bow, many of the early ones retained theirs to the war's end. The *Hornet* is launching her aircraft over the stern, an uncommon event, as witness the large audience crowding the island.

A damaged Avenger aircraft has just landed on the *Essex*. Shown to good effect is the flight deck expansion joint by the tailwheel and the slotted plate that allows the crash barrier wires to lie flush with the flight deck.

Showing just how tight the flight deck could be, an *Essex* is about to launch her air group. Seen here are about forty-plus aircraft (50 percent of the total complement). The remainder are probably in the process of being launched from the bow catapults. (Official U.S. Navy photograph)

Six of the early units were fitted with an athwartships hangar deck catapult. Used only rarely, these catapults were removed in the 1944 refits and an additional flight deck catapult fitted. This one is seen at the moment of launch. (National Archives)

Hellcats being launched from the *Randolph* in July 1945. By war's end, up to 40 percent of all launchings were by catapult. (Official U.S. Navy photograph)

Seen at Ulithi in December 1944 are six of the *Essex* class. In the front
row (from nearest the camera) are the *Wasp, Yorktown, Hornet, Hancock,*
and *Ticonderoga;* in the row behind is the *Lexington.* These ships were the
epitome of the U.S. Navy's offensive power in World War II. (Official U.S.
Navy photograph)

The aircraft carrier was always the kamikazes' most important target, and many were damaged by them in the last eleven months of the war. Although this sort of damage appeared dramatic, as in this picture of the *Ticonderoga* after the plane has hit the island, it could be repaired at a forward base or at Pearl Harbor, and more important, the ship could still operate aircraft while in this damaged condition. (Official U.S. Navy photograph)

In March 1945 the *Randolph* was hit by a kamikaze aft on the flight deck. Damage was not enough to send her to the mainland for repairs, and the damage was made good at Ulithi.

The *Lexington* receiving oil from a tanker while operating as part of TG 58.2 in the China Sea in January 1945. She was one of the first to receive the three outboard 40-mm mounts slung below the island at the forecastle. The mounts were fitted in February 1944 on the West Coast during repairs. Just visible is the Mk 49 director with the associated Mk 11 radar located between the two forward 40-mm mounts on the fore end of the island.

In May 1945 the *Bunker Hill* was hit by two kamikazes and suffered extensive damage. Repairs were completed in late July 1945, too late for her to see further combat. She took part in Operation Magic Carpet until placed in reserve in January 1947. She never returned to service but acted as a static floating test bed for electronic equipment until the early 1980s. The broadside view of the island shows her updated rig following repairs to battle damage, with the SM radar replaced with SP and the SC replaced with SR, while the rear view of the island shows that the Mk 51 directors for the island 40-mm mounts have been replaced with Mk 63s. The aftermost director is coupled with a Mk 28 radar, the antenna being fitted to the barrels of the aftermost quadruple 40-mm mount. (National Archives)

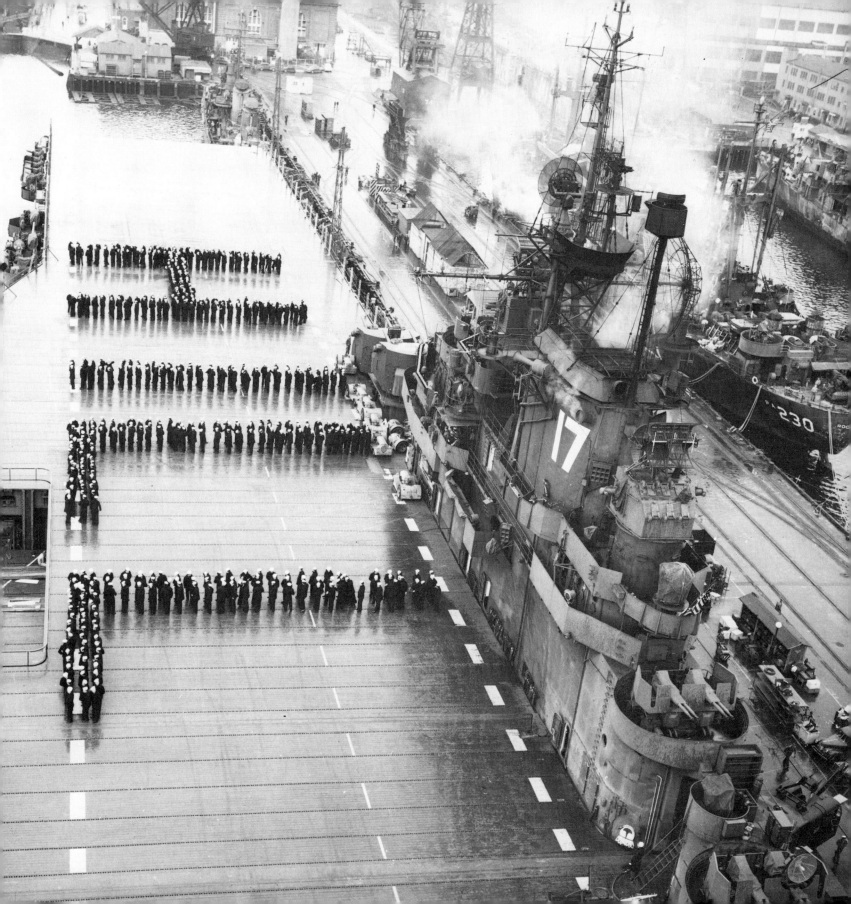

A vertical aerial view of the *Lexington* taken in March 1944.

A broadside picture of the *Lexington* taken upon completion of a West Coast refit in May 1945. During this refit she was fitted with twin 20-mm mountings and six 0.5-inch quadruple machine gun mountings (see the general arrangement plans for location).

The starboard side of the *Essex*'s island in August 1943. A second SG radar has been fitted on the mainmast, and the SC radar raised on a tall lattice tower outboard of the funnel. (Official U.S. Navy photograph)

The *Essex* in April 1944 upon completion of a refit in San Francisco. Changes to the rig are as follows: the SK moved to the starboard side of the funnel; the SM on the fore end of the foremast platform; the SC fitted aft of the platform; the second SG moved and placed on top of the lattice tower on the port side of the funnel; and the mainmast removed. (National Archives)

In February 1944 the *Lexington* was fitted experimentally for a short period with a zenith search radar, SO 11. Only four of these were ever fitted to ships, and the other three went to battleships. The antenna can be seen at the top of the pole mainmast. The performance was disappointing, and the set was removed and replaced with an SG set after a few months.

The *Yorktown* was the only ship of the class to carry an SK radar on the port side of the funnel. This photo shows the installation taking place at Ulithi in May 1945.

The island of the *Hornet*, taken in August 1944. In the background at left is the *Essex*.

On board the *Boxer* on 31 March 1945. As with vessels completing at this time, the SC has been supplanted with SR, and the *Boxer* was the first ship of the class to receive the SP, with the six-foot cut antenna carried just forward of the foretopmast.

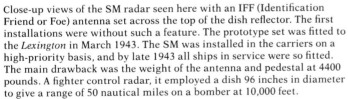

Close-up views of the SM radar seen here with an IFF (Identification Friend or Foe) antenna set across the top of the dish reflector. The first installations were without such a feature. The prototype set was fitted to the *Lexington* in March 1943. The SM was installed in the carriers on a high-priority basis, and by late 1943 all ships in service were so fitted. The main drawback was the weight of the antenna and pedestal at 4400 pounds. A fighter control radar, it employed a dish 96 inches in diameter to give a range of 50 nautical miles on a bomber at 10,000 feet.

Wartime Drawings

A. General Arrangement Plans

General arrangement plans for the USS *Essex* as she appeared in August 1943 showing initial modifications made to the rig. The flight deck drawing does not show the planking or the tie-down metal strips; these have been omitted for reasons of clarity, thus allowing the arrester wires and crash barriers to be clearly shown. The *Essex* is especially interesting in that she was fitted for astern launch and bow retrieval of aircraft and shows this in the wire arrangement carried right up to the bow. The tie-down strip arrangement is identical to those shown for the *Lexington*.

A special attempt was made to show precisely the various heights of the gallery deck platform and the ladders and openings alongside. The body plan, although strictly applicable to the long-bow units, can be used for the short-bow vessels; the only difference is at the extreme bow.

USS *Essex*—Starboard Outboard Profile

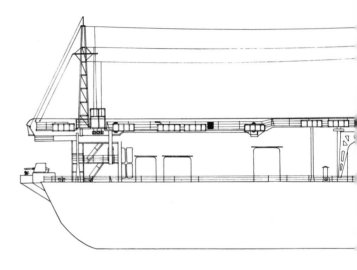

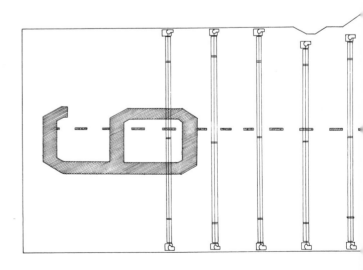

USS *Essex*—Flight Deck

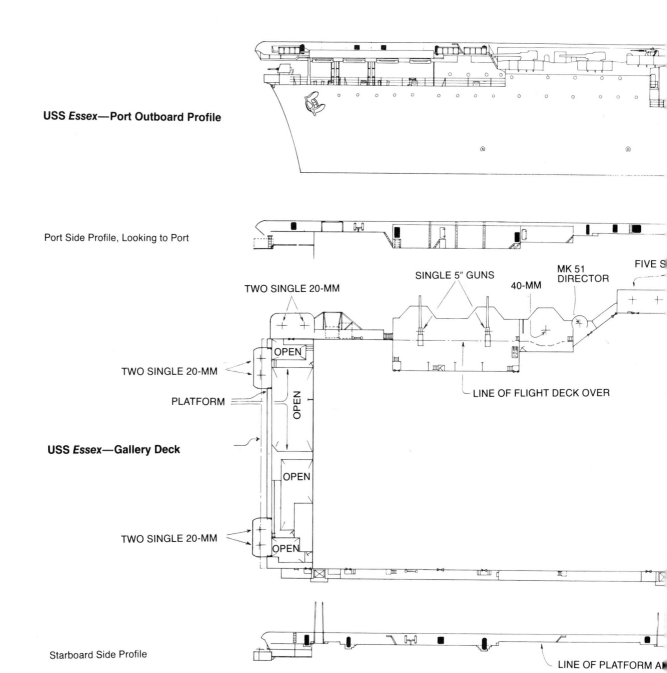

USS _Essex_—Port Outboard Profile

Port Side Profile, Looking to Port

SINGLE 5" GUNS

MK 51
DIRECTOR

FIVE S

40-MM

TWO SINGLE 20-MM

TWO SINGLE 20-MM

PLATFORM

OPEN

OPEN

OPEN

LINE OF FLIGHT DECK OVER

USS _Essex_—Gallery Deck

OPEN

TWO SINGLE 20-MM

OPEN

Starboard Side Profile

LINE OF PLATFORM A

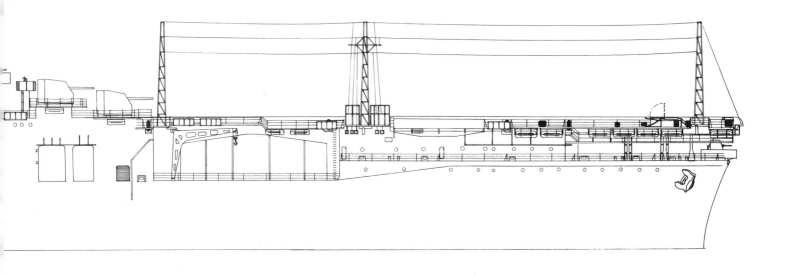

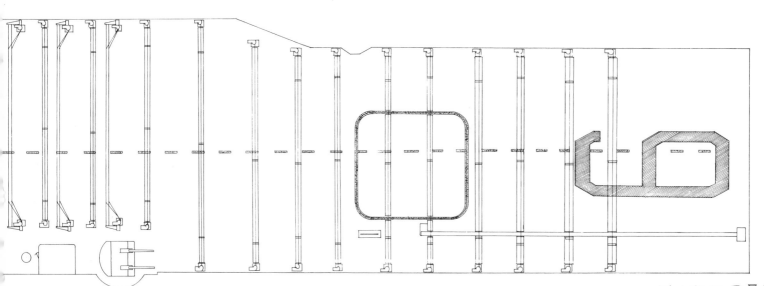

FLIGHT DECK

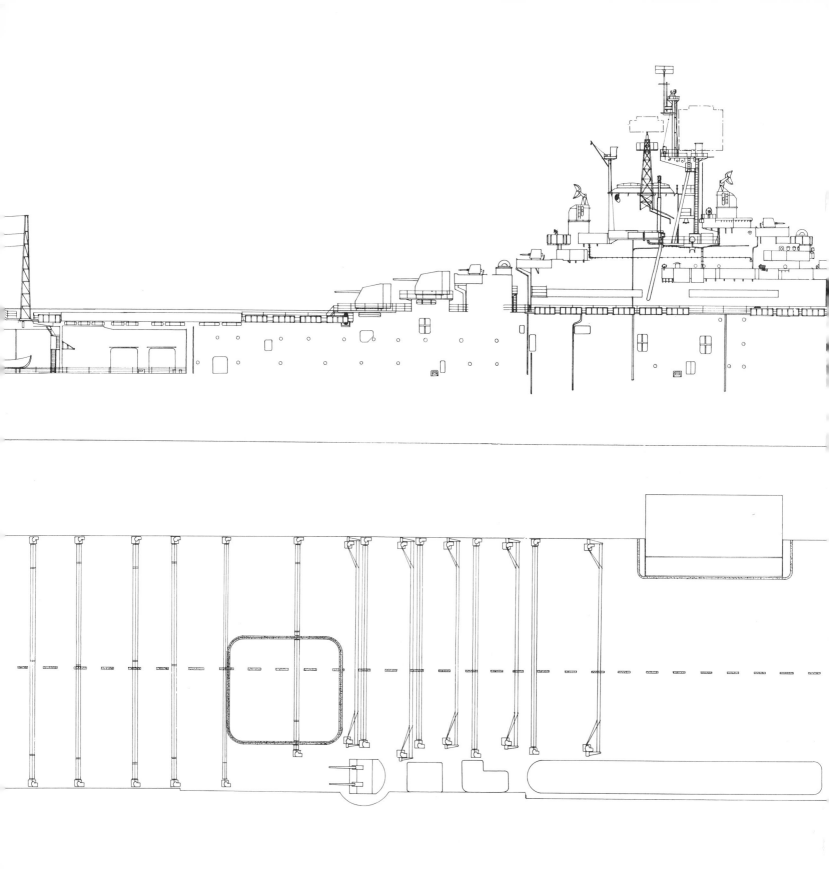

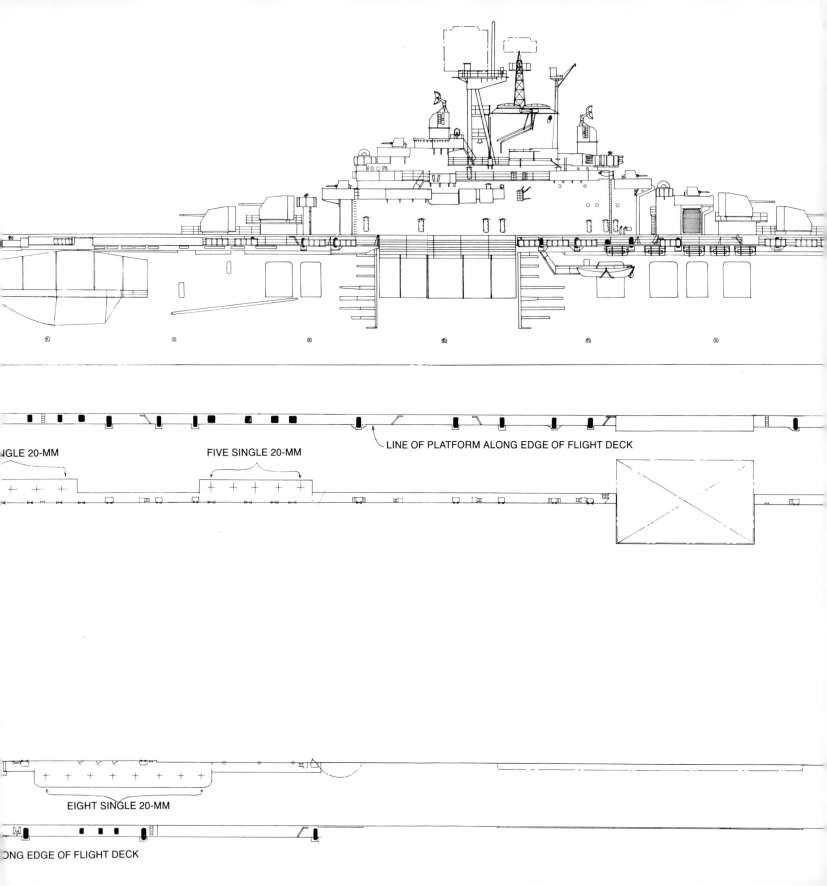

NGLE 20-MM

FIVE SINGLE 20-MM

LINE OF PLATFORM ALONG EDGE OF FLIGHT DECK

EIGHT SINGLE 20-MM

ONG EDGE OF FLIGHT DECK

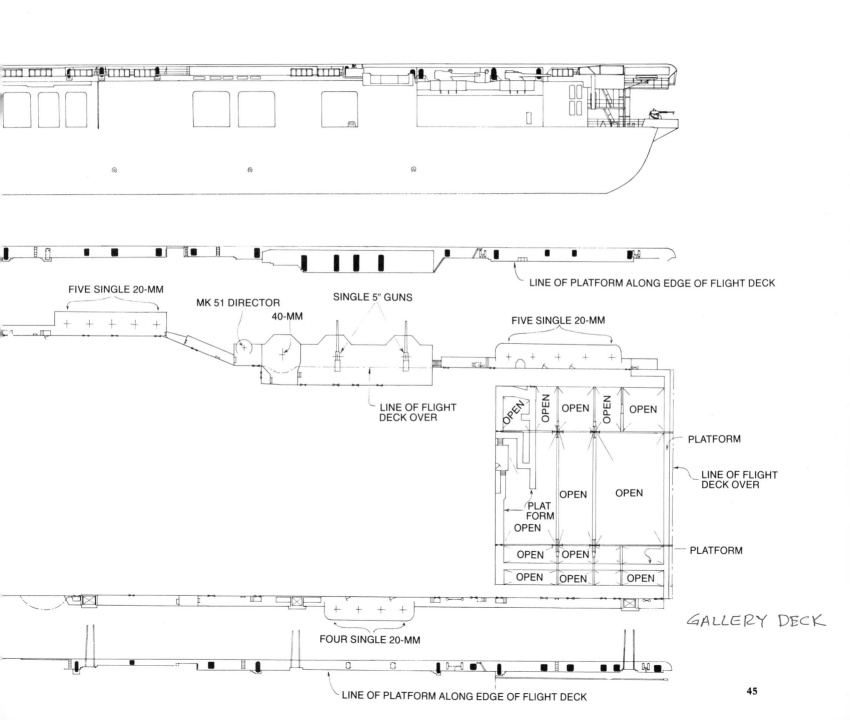

FIVE SINGLE 20-MM

MK 51 DIRECTOR

40-MM

SINGLE 5" GUNS

FIVE SINGLE 20-MM

LINE OF PLATFORM ALONG EDGE OF FLIGHT DECK

LINE OF FLIGHT
DECK OVER

OPEN

OPEN

OPEN

OPEN

OPEN

PLATFORM

LINE OF FLIGHT
DECK OVER

OPEN

OPEN

PLAT
FORM
OPEN

OPEN

OPEN

PLATFORM

OPEN

OPEN

OPEN

FOUR SINGLE 20-MM

GALLERY DECK

LINE OF PLATFORM ALONG EDGE OF FLIGHT DECK

45

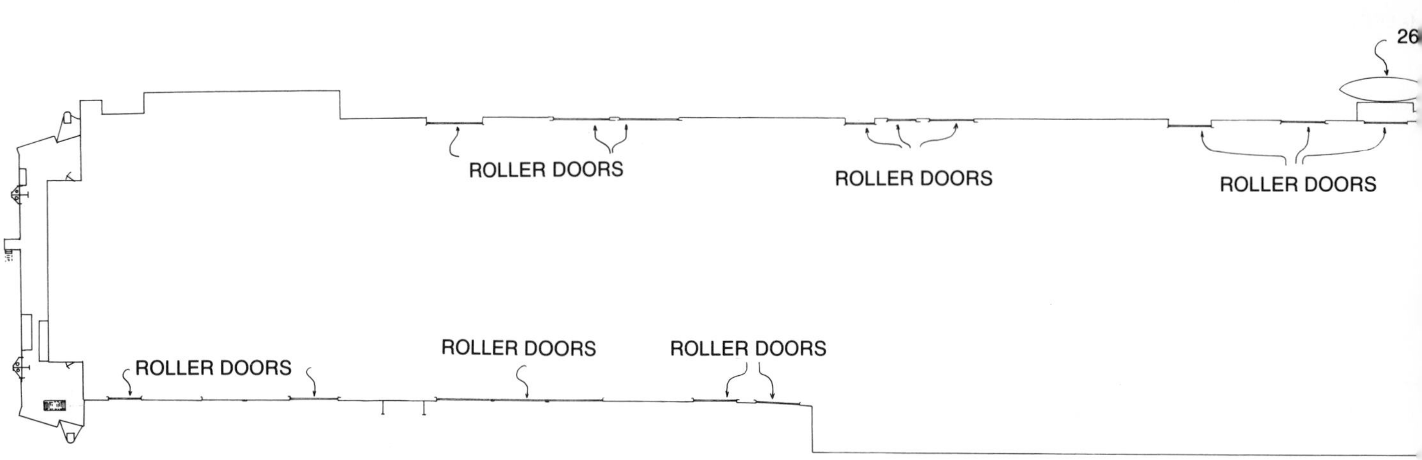

26

ROLLER DOORS

ROLLER DOORS

ROLLER DOORS

ROLLER DOORS

ROLLER DOORS

ROLLER DOORS

ROLLER DOORS

USS *Essex*—Forecastle Deck

HALEBOAT

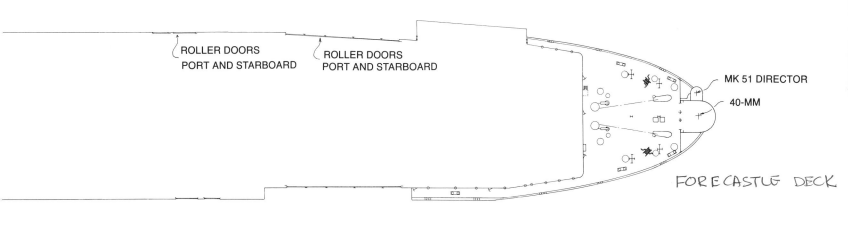

ROLLER DOORS
PORT AND STARBOARD

ROLLER DOORS
PORT AND STARBOARD

MK 51 DIRECTOR

40-MM

FORECASTLE DECK

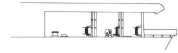

Bow Profile at Forecastle Deck Level

USS *Essex*

Key to Bridge Decks
1. Radar repair room
2. Flag radio
3. Flag radio
4. Admiral's sea cabin
5. 20-mm ready service room
6. Uptakes
7. Aerological office
8. Flag plot
9. Radar control room
10. Radar plot
11. 40-mm ready service room
12. Pilothouse
13. Chart house
14. Air plot
15. Radar room
16. Radar control room
17. 20-mm ready service room

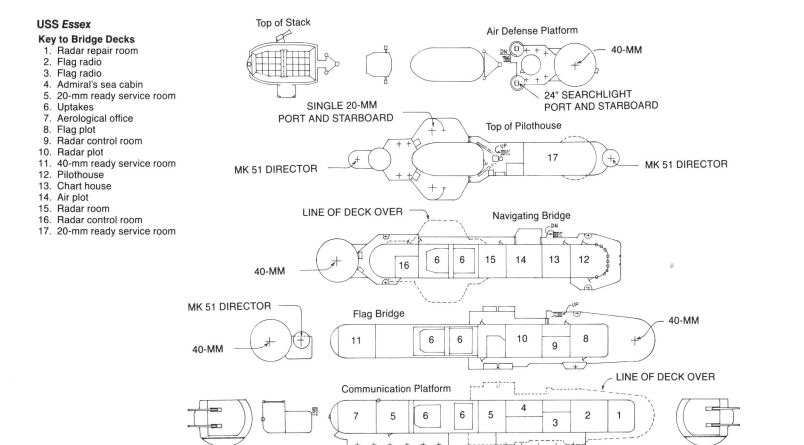

Top of Stack

Air Defense Platform

40-MM

DN

24" SEARCHLIGHT
PORT AND STARBOARD

SINGLE 20-MM
PORT AND STARBOARD

Top of Pilothouse

UP

17

MK 51 DIRECTOR

MK 51 DIRECTOR

LINE OF DECK OVER

Navigating Bridge

DN

40-MM

| 16 | 6 | 6 | 15 | 14 | 13 | 12 |

MK 51 DIRECTOR

Flag Bridge

UP

40-MM

| 11 | 6 | 6 | | 10 | 9 | 8 |

40-MM

40-MM

LINE OF DECK OVER

Communication Platform

LINE OF DECK OVER

| 7 | 5 | 6 | 6 | 5 | 4 | 3 | 2 | 1 |

SIX SINGLE 20-MM

FIVE SINGLE 20-MM

USS *Essex*—Inboard Profile

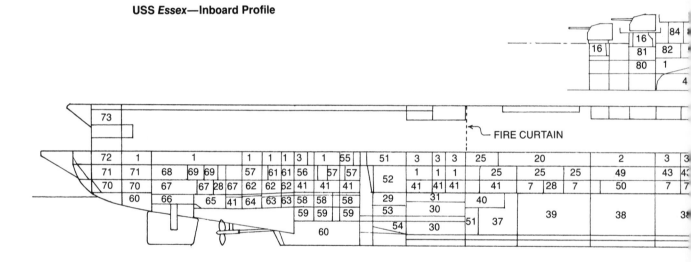

FIRE CURTAIN

Key to Inboard Profile

1. Crew's berthing
2. Junior officers' bunk room
3. Showers
4. Linen locker
5. 40-mm ready room
6. Boatswain's stores
7. Stores
8. Windlass room
9. Peak tank
10. Chain locker
11. Pump room
12. Forward emergency generator room
13. Link belt stowage
14. Incendiary bombs
15. 20-mm aircraft ammunition
16. 5" handling room
17. Elevator machinery and pump room
18. Catapult pump space
19. Catapult machinery
20. Elevator pit
21. Gas tank
22. Lube oil and pump room
23. Aircraft ammunition stowage
24. Catapult machinery
25. Passage and messroom
26. Wardroom and messroom
27. Wardroom and stateroom
28. Trunk
29. Gas pump motor room
30. Gas tank
31. Bomb stowage
32. Pantry
33. Galley
34. Bomb fuse magazine
35. Combat Information Center (CIC)
36. 20-mm aircraft magazine
37. Auxiliary machinery room
38. Boiler room
39. Engine room
40. 5" powder room
41. Aviation stores
42. Marines' berthing
43. General workshops
44. Barbershop
45. Uptake space
46. Engineer's office
47. Navigator's office
48. Supply office
49. Crew's galley
50. Laundry
51. Torpedo workshop
52. Torpedo stowage
53. 40-mm magazine
54. 20-mm magazine

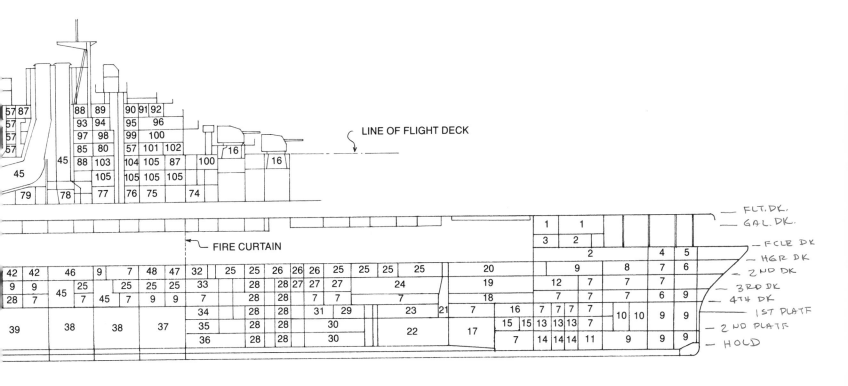

LINE OF FLIGHT DECK

FIRE CURTAIN

55. Carpenter's shop
56. Operations room
57. Passage
58. Perishable stores
59. Refrigeration machinery room
60. Void
61. CPO's pantry
62. Aft emergency diesel generator room
63. Meat room
64. Thaw room
65. Motor control room
66. Steering gear room
67. Aviation engine stowage
68. CPO's washroom
69. Uniform stores
70. CPO's showers and WC
71. Engineer's stores
72. Capstan machinery room

73. Aviation engine and propeller shop
74. Compressor room
75. Chemical mixing room
76. Print room
77. Copy room
78. Battery storage room
79. Trash burner room
80. Crew's WC
81. Flight deck gear
82. Optical repair room
83. 40-mm ready service room
84. Pilot balloon room
85. Squadron locker
86. Aerological office
87. Radar control room
88. Radar room
89. Air plot
90. Chart house

91. Captain's sea cabin
92. Pilothouse
93. Flag officer's sea cabin
94. Transmitting room
95. VHF radio room
96. Flag plot
97. 20-mm ready service room
98. Admiral's sea cabin
99. Flag office
100. Radio room
101. Flight deck crew
102. Flight deck control
103. Radio intelligence
104. Commander's station
105. Coding room
106. Captain's stateroom

USS *Essex*

Key to 2nd, 3rd, and 4th Decks
1. Windlass room
2. Cabin
3. Stores
4. Elevator pit
5. Fan room
6. Pantry
7. Wardroom and messroom
8. Wardroom lounge
9. Navigator's office
10. Flag office
11. Supply office
12. Supply office
13. Executive officer's office
14. Captain's office
15. Gunnery office
16. Damage control office
17. Elevator machinery space
18. Vent trunk
19. Engineer's office
20. Trash burner
21. Uptakes
22. Officers' WC
23. Marines' berthing
24. Uniform locker
25. Crew's WC
26. Marines' WC
27. Marines' stores
28. Repair locker
29. Coat locker
30. Crew's berthing
31. Uptakes
32. Garbage disposal
33. 5" handling room
34. Crew's library
35. Carpenter's shop
36. Torpedo workshop
37. Capstan room
38. Inert material
39. Emergency diesel generator room
40. Catapult machinery
41. Canvas and fabric workshop
42. Warrant officer's messroom
43. Crew's mess
44. Bomb vane stowage
45. Pantry
46. General workshop
47. Print shop
48. Electrical workshop
49. Crew's galley
50. Butcher shop
51. Bakery
52. Sick bay
53. CPO's mess
54. CPO's berthing
55. Torpedo stowage
56. Dental office
57. Catapult pump space
58. Armory
59. Pump room
60. Aviation stores
61. Barber shop
62. Laundry
63. Dry provisions
64. Main issue room
65. Torpedo stowage

2nd Deck

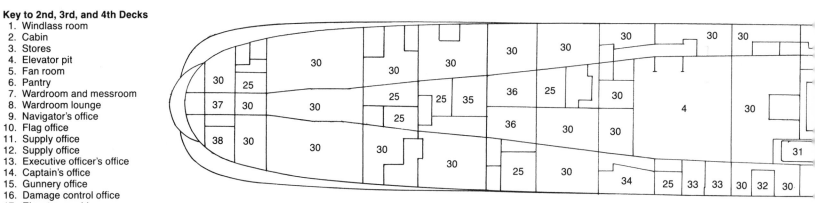

3rd Deck

4th Deck

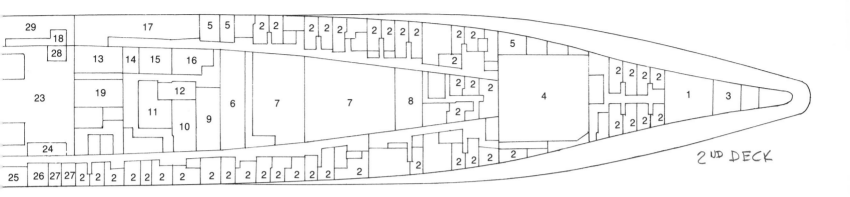

2ᴺᴰ DECK

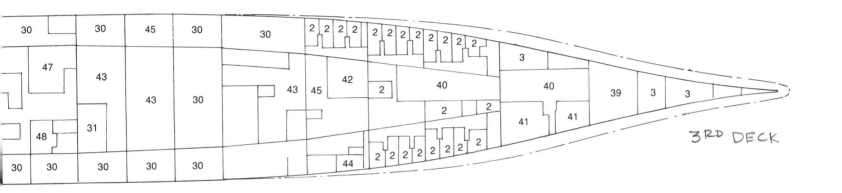

3ᴿᴰ DECK

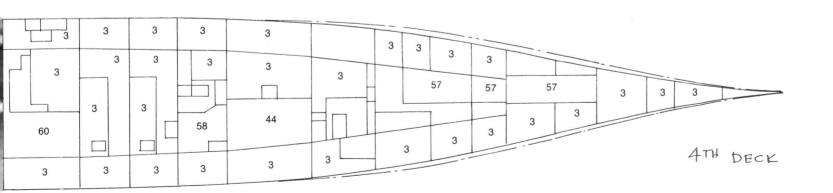

4TH DECK

USS *Essex*

1st Platform Deck

Key to 1st and 2nd Platform Decks and Hold
1. Stores
2. Ordnance stores
3. Fuel oil
4. Projectile stowage
5. 5" handling room
6. 5" powder room
7. 40-mm magazine
8. Bomb stowage
9. Generator flat
10. Boiler room
11. Engine room
12. Torpedo stowage
13. Perishable stores
14. Aviation stores
15. Motor control room
16. Steering gear room
17. Link belt stowage
18. Pyrotechnics stowage
19. Elevator machinery room
20. 20-mm aircraft ammunition
21. 50-caliber magazine
22. Bomb stowage
23. Gas tank
24. Damage control
25. Central station
26. Plotting station
27. IC room
28. Auxiliary machinery room
29. 20-mm magazine
30. CIC

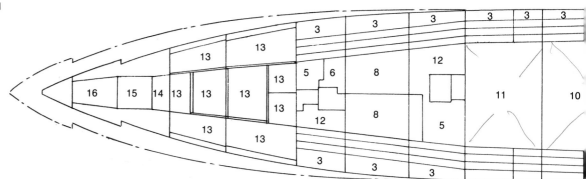

2nd Platform Deck

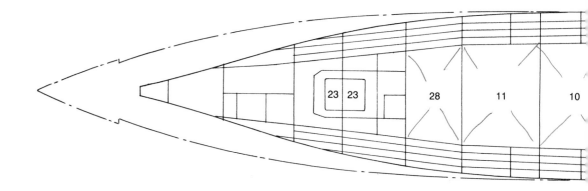

Hold

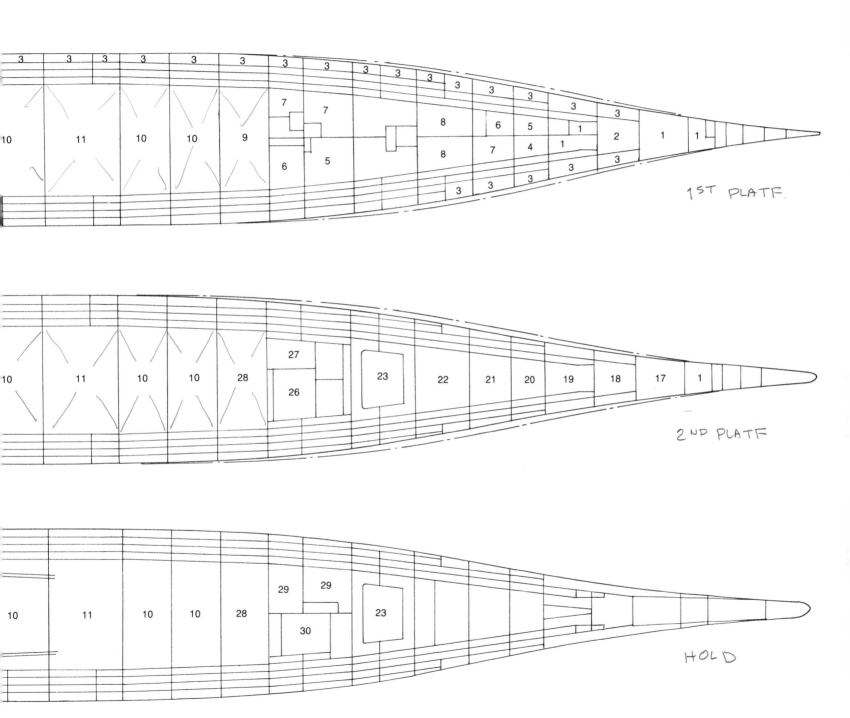

1ST PLATF.

2ND PLATF

HOLD

Frame 175

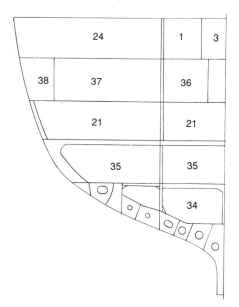

Frame 114

Frame 104 (Upper Half)

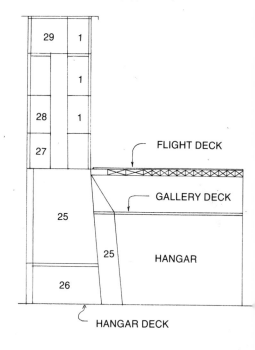

FLIGHT DECK

GALLERY DECK

HANGAR

HANGAR DECK

BOILER ROOM

USS *Essex*—Sections

Key to Sections

1. Passage
2. Wardroom and stateroom
3. Showers
4. Passage
5. Emergency diesel generator room
6. Stores
7. Link belt stowage
8. Incendiary bombs
9. Gasoline tank
10. Void
11. Fuel oil
12. Wiring trunk
13. Bomb stowage
14. Trunk
15. Cells
16. Bomb elevator
17. Air objective folder stowage
18. Bomb vane stowage
19. Crew's mess
20. Wardroom and messroom
21. Aviation stores
22. Print shop
23. Marines' berthing
24. Crew's berthing
25. Uptake
26. Trash burner room
27. Repair room
28. Aerological room
29. Radar control room
30. Fire brick stowage
31. Crew's WC
32. General workshop
33. Dry provisions
34. Film storage
35. Fruit and vegetables
36. Surgical rooms
37. Surgical dressing room
38. Battle dressing stores

Frame 104 (Lower Half)

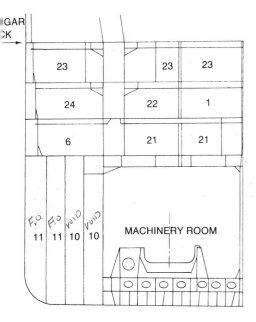

GAR
CK →

23	23	23
24	22	1
6	21	21

F.O. 11 | F.O 11 | VOID 10 | VOID 10

MACHINERY ROOM

Frame 62

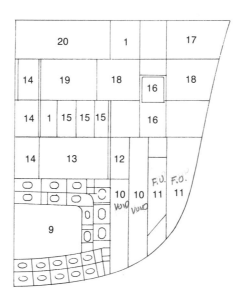

20	1	17
14	19	18	16	18
14	1	15	15	15	16
14	13	12

9

10 | 10 | 11 | 11
VOID | VOID | F.O. | F.O.

Frame 23

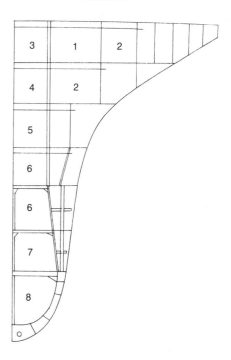

3	1	2
4	2	
5		
6		
6		
7		
8		

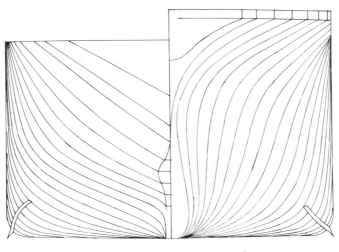

Body Plan (Long-Hull Type)

USS *Randolph*—Starboard Outboard Profile

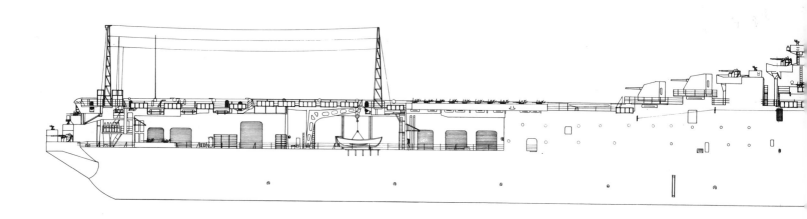

General arrangement plans for the USS *Randolph* (a long-bow unit) as in late 1944 as completed, with ten 40-mm quadruple Mk 2 mountings and fifty-seven single 20-mm Mk 10 mountings.

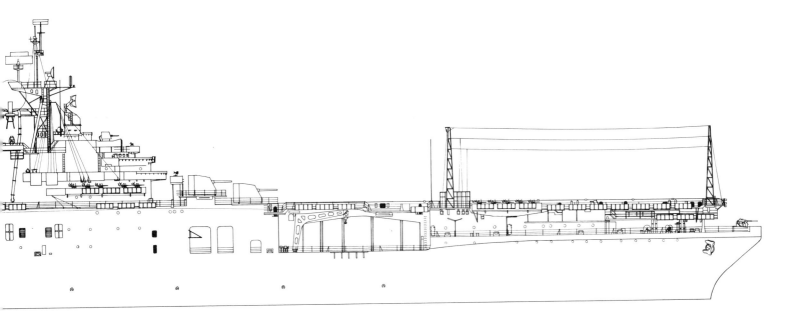

USS *Randolph*—Port Outboard Profile

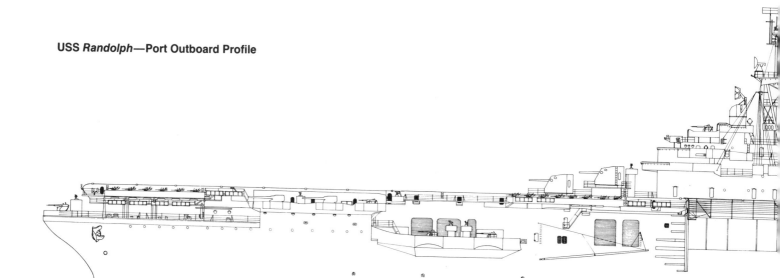

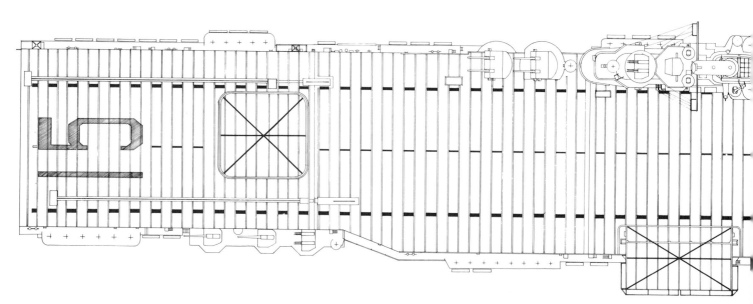

USS *Randolph*—Flight Deck

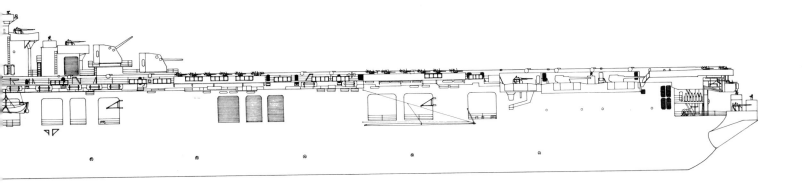

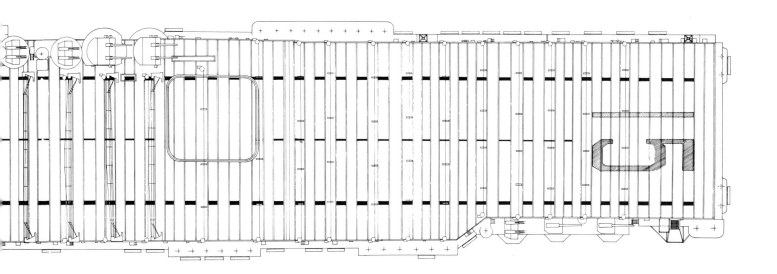

General arrangement plans for the USS *Lexington* as refitted in May 1945. Typical of many vessels at the war's end, she now has seventeen quadruple 40-mm mounts, including three below the island to starboard. The single 20-mms have been replaced by twins, and six quadruple 0.5-inch machine guns have been installed. Her rig shows an important change with the fitting of SR air search radar in place of the SC-2 outfit.

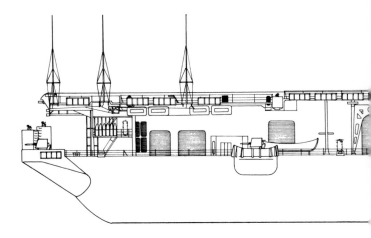

Key to Flight Deck
1. 5″ handling room
2. Flight deck control
3. Flight deck crew
4. Ammunition hoist
5. Crew's WC
6. Emergency dressing station
7. Uptakes
8. Repair shop
9. Squadron lockers
10. Pilot balloon room

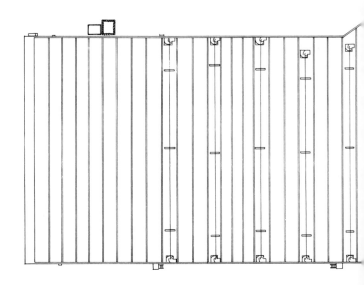

USS *Lexington*—Flight Deck

Key to Gallery Deck

1. Crew's berthing
2. Crew's washroom and WC
3. 5" handling room
4. Crew's locker room
5. Radio transmitter room
6. Radio workshop
7. Elevator trunk
8. Aircraft ammunition stowage
9. 20-mm ready room
10. Captain's cabin
11. Passage
12. Admiral's cabin
13. Admiral's stateroom
14. Galley
15. Gas line gear locker
16. Mk 29 radar room
17. Stores
18. Gun cleaning room
19. Flight deck lighting control
20. Squadron armory
21. Captain's pantry
22. Staff office
23. Senior staff office
24. Captain's office
25. Captain's stateroom
26. CIC
27. Air plot
28. Squadron workshop
29. Radar room
30. Aviation radar room
31. Tool issue room
32. Electric service station
33. Squadron ready room
34. Squadron office
35. Squadron service room
36. Air intelligence room
37. Elevator stowing machinery
38. Radar room
39. Lobby
40. Air group commander's ready room
41. WCs
42. Lockers
43. Uptakes
44. 20-mm ready room
45. Tool room
46. Drop tank stowage
47. Radar bomb stowage rack
48. Air conditioning equipment room
49. Air ammunition belting room
50. 40-mm ready room
51. 20-mm workshop
52. Parachute packing space
53. Stowage
54. 40-mm workshop
55. 40-mm gun control and Mk 29 radar
56. Aft radio station
57. Aviation engine repair shop
58. Arrester gear spare parts and repair shop

USS *Lexington*—Port Outboard Profile

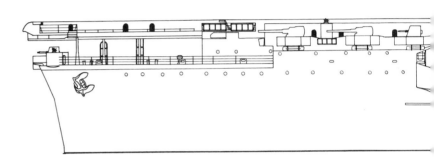

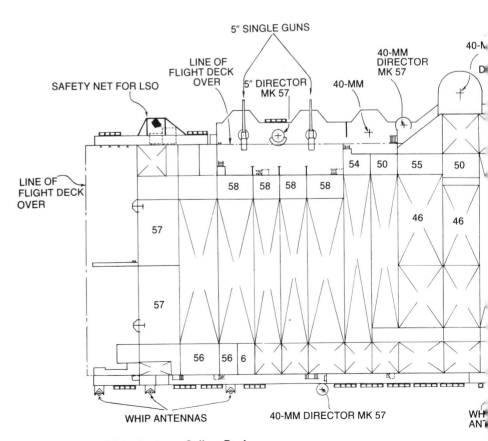

USS *Lexington*—Gallery Deck

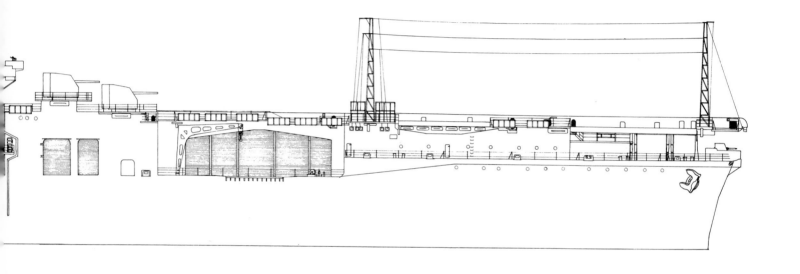

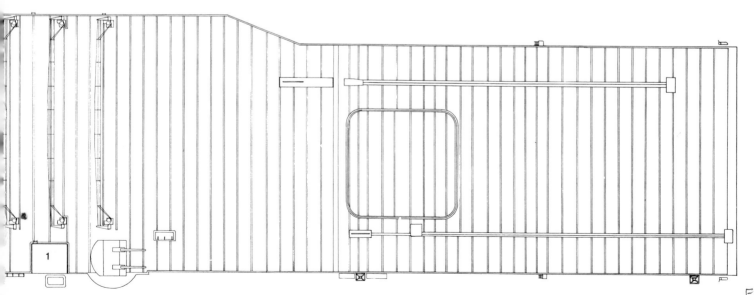

FLT. DK

61

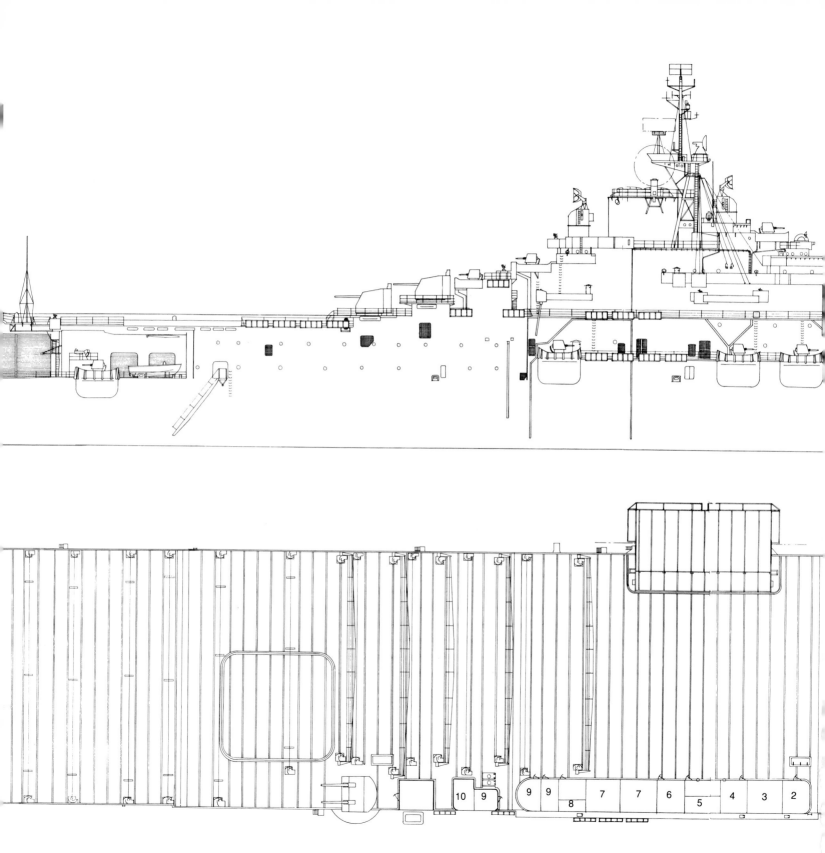

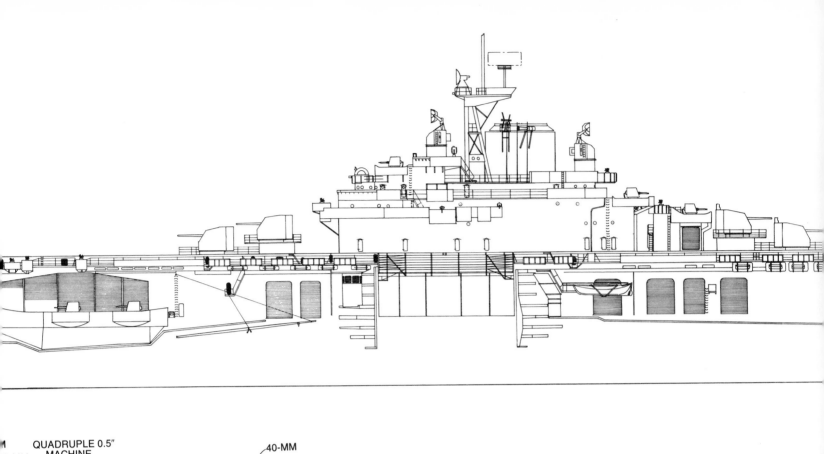

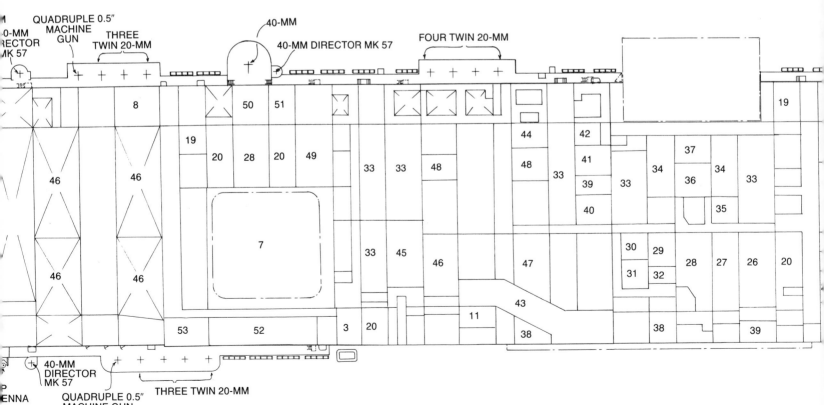

QUADRUPLE 0.5"
MACHINE
GUN

THREE
TWIN 20-MM

-MM
RECTOR
MK 57

40-MM

40-MM DIRECTOR MK 57

FOUR TWIN 20-MM

40-MM
DIRECTOR
MK 57

THREE TWIN 20-MM

QUADRUPLE 0.5"
MACHINE GUN

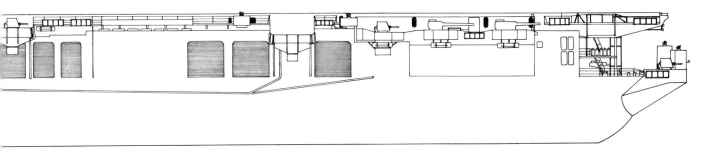

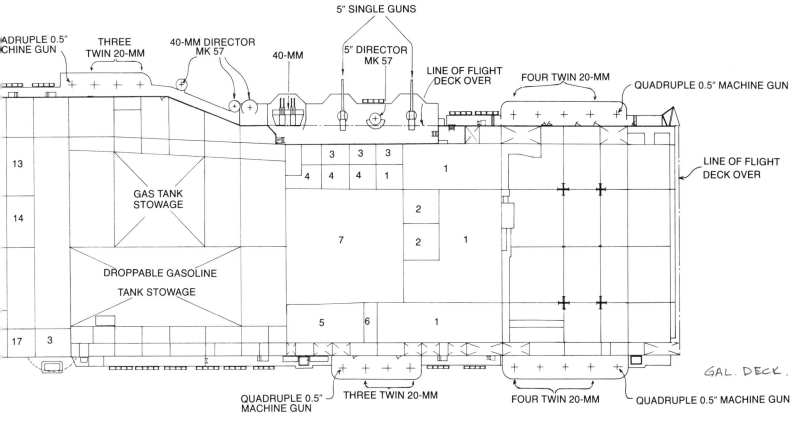

5" SINGLE GUNS

40-MM DIRECTOR
MK 57

40-MM

5" DIRECTOR
MK 57

LINE OF FLIGHT
DECK OVER

FOUR TWIN 20-MM

QUADRUPLE 0.5" MACHINE GUN

ADRUPLE 0.5"
CHINE GUN

THREE
TWIN 20-MM

LINE OF FLIGHT
DECK OVER

GAS TANK
STOWAGE

DROPPABLE GASOLINE
TANK STOWAGE

13

14

17   3

3   3   3   1

4   4   4   1

2

7   2   1

5   6   1

QUADRUPLE 0.5"
MACHINE GUN

THREE TWIN 20-MM

FOUR TWIN 20-MM

QUADRUPLE 0.5" MACHINE GUN

GAL. DECK.

Key to Forecastle Deck
1. Junior officers' bunk room
2. Cabins
3. Staff office
4. Washroom and showers
5. Uptake
6. Projection room
7. Engineer maintenance office
8. Elevator trunk
9. Deck edge elevator
10. Hangar deck equipment
11. Crew's berthing
12. Crew's WC
13. 40-mm practice loading machine
14. Ready service aircraft parts and issue room
15. Oxygen transfer room
16. Carpenter's shop

Key to Hangar Deck
1. Cabins
2. Junior officers' bunk room
3. Washroom and WCs
4. Stores
5. Elevator opening
6. Roller curtain
7. Uptake
8. Printing and developing rooms
9. Copying room
10. Storage battery shop
11. WC
12. Battery workshop
13. Trash burner
14. Trash bin
15. Hangar deck equipment
16. Blacksmith shop
17. Aviation repair shop
18. Diving gear
19. Crew's berthing
20. 40-mm ready room
21. Vent trunk
22. Aviation tool room
23. Aviation repair shop
24. Torpedo hatch
25. Fueling gear locker
26. 26' motor whaleboat
27. Bomb elevator

Key to Bridge Decks
1. Radio and flag room
2. Radar room
3. 20-mm ready room
4. Uptake
5. 20-mm ready room
6. Aerological office
7. Flag office
8. Staff office
9. Admiral's sea cabin
10. Cabin
11. Flight deck amplifier equipment
12. 40-mm ready room
13. Pilot balloon room
14. Pilothouse
15. Chart house
16. Air center
17. Wiring trunk

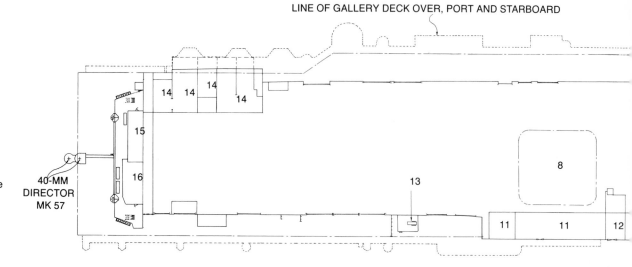

USS *Lexington*—Forecastle Deck

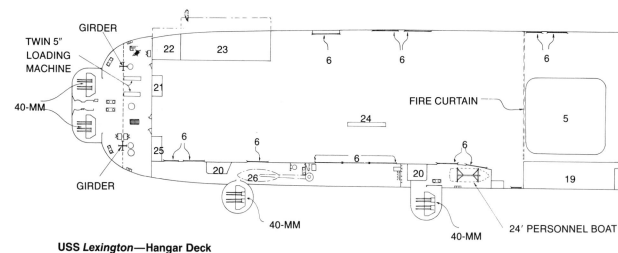

USS *Lexington*—Hangar Deck

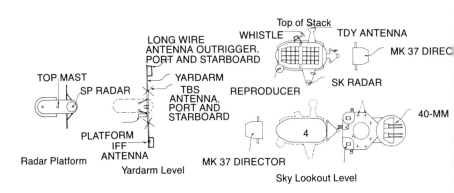

USS *Lexington*—Island Platforms

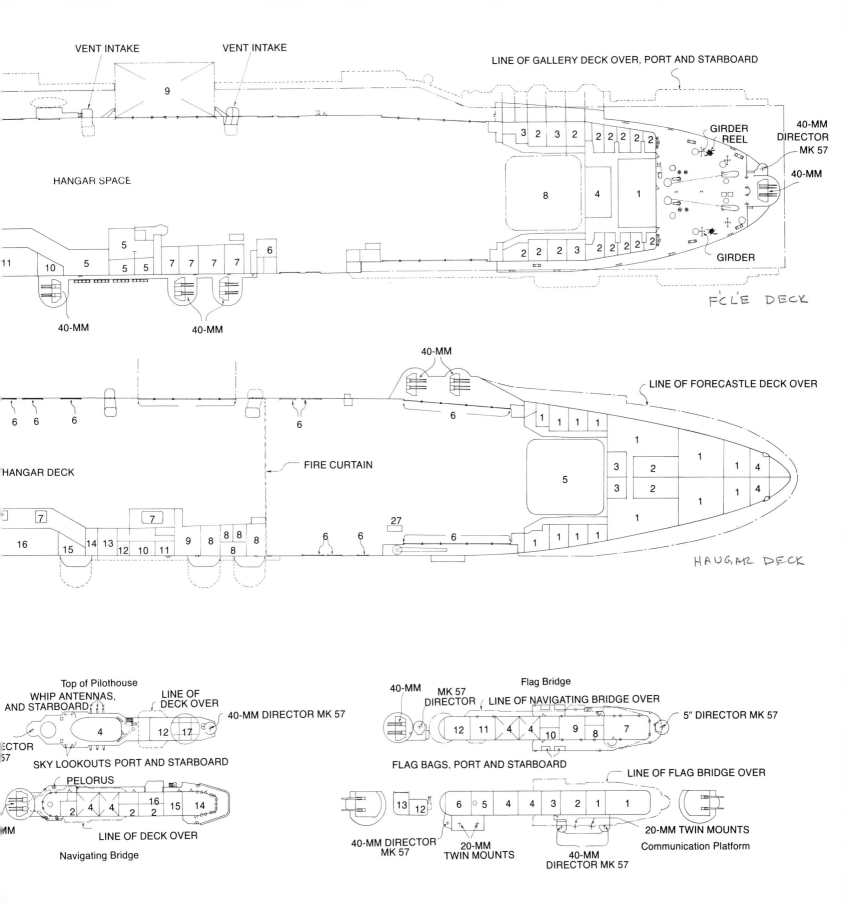

VENT INTAKE   VENT INTAKE

LINE OF GALLERY DECK OVER, PORT AND STARBOARD

9

HANGAR SPACE

GIRDER REEL

40-MM DIRECTOR MK 57

40-MM

3 2 3 2 2 2 2 2 2

8   4   1

5

5 5 5 6

11 10 5 5 5 7 7 7 7

2 2 2 3 2 2 2 2 2

GIRDER

F'C'L'E DECK

40-MM   40-MM

40-MM

LINE OF FORECASTLE DECK OVER

6

1 1 1

1

HANGAR DECK

FIRE CURTAIN

3 2 1 1 4

5

3 2 1 1 4

1

27

7   7

6 6 6

16 15 14 13 12 10 11 9 8 8 8 8 8

6 6 6   6

1 1 1 1

HAUGAR DECK

Top of Pilothouse
WHIP ANTENNAS,
AND STARBOARD

LINE OF DECK OVER

40-MM DIRECTOR MK 57

4   12 17

ECTOR 57

SKY LOOKOUTS PORT AND STARBOARD

PELORUS

2 4 4 2 16 15 14

LINE OF DECK OVER

Navigating Bridge

40-MM

MK 57 DIRECTOR

Flag Bridge

LINE OF NAVIGATING BRIDGE OVER

5" DIRECTOR MK 57

12 11 4 4 10 9 8 7

FLAG BAGS, PORT AND STARBOARD

LINE OF FLAG BRIDGE OVER

13 12

6 5 4 4 3 2 1 1

20-MM TWIN MOUNTS

40-MM DIRECTOR MK 57

20-MM TWIN MOUNTS

40-MM DIRECTOR MK 57

Communication Platform

B. Rig Configurations

Tripod Foremast

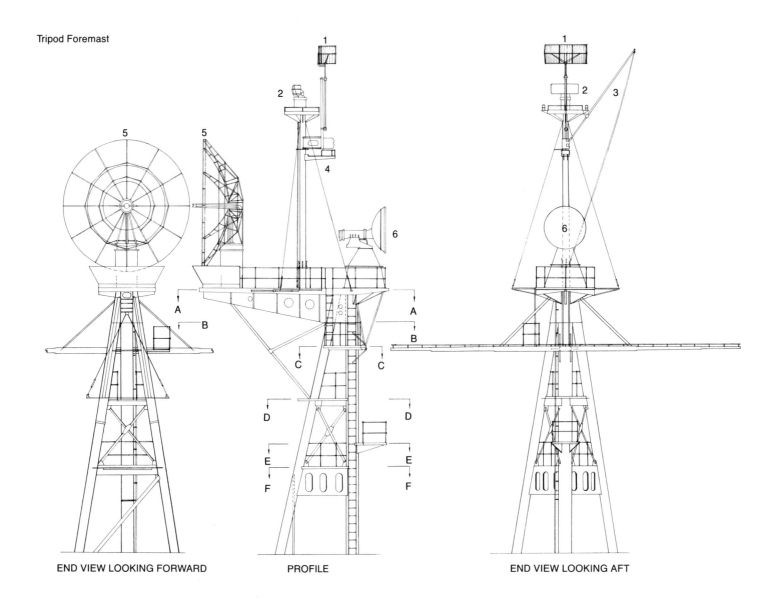

END VIEW LOOKING FORWARD   PROFILE   END VIEW LOOKING AFT

Key to Tripod Rig Arrangement
1. YE homing beacon
2. SG radar antenna
3. Ensign staff
4. Servicing platform
5. SK or SK-2 radar antenna
6. SM or SP radar antenna

Profile, end, and plan views of the tripod foremast as fitted to the *Hornet*, *Franklin*, *Hancock*, *Intrepid*, *Ticonderoga*, *Shangri-La*, and *Bennington*. The first five were fitted with SK and not SK-2 as shown in the drawing, while the *Shangri-La* and *Bennington* were fitted as per the drawings for only a few weeks before the SK-2 was moved to a position outboard of the funnel and the SC put in its place.

The drawings, although accurate, should be used for guidance to varying degrees for most of the class as they appeared in the war.

Tripod Foremast Platforms

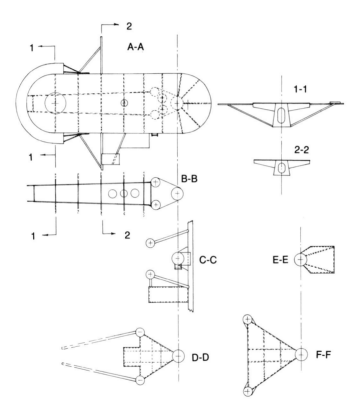

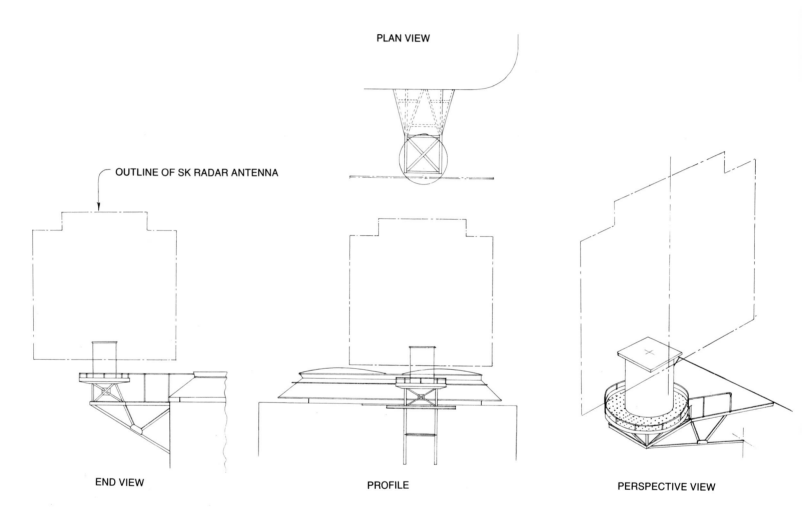

PLAN VIEW

OUTLINE OF SK RADAR ANTENNA

END VIEW

PROFILE

PERSPECTIVE VIEW

Details for the SK platform originally used for SC radar.

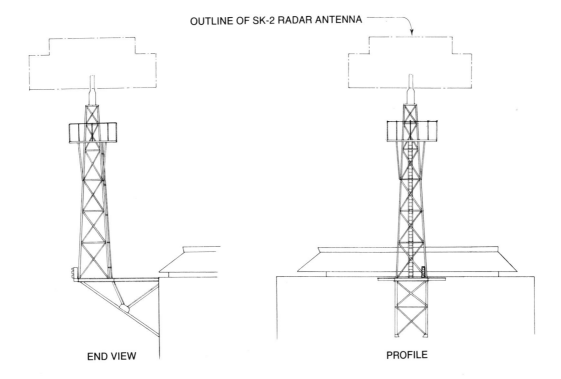

OUTLINE OF SK-2 RADAR ANTENNA

END VIEW   PROFILE

Details of the lattice mast to carry the SC radar or sometimes the SG radar. This mast could be fitted port or starboard.

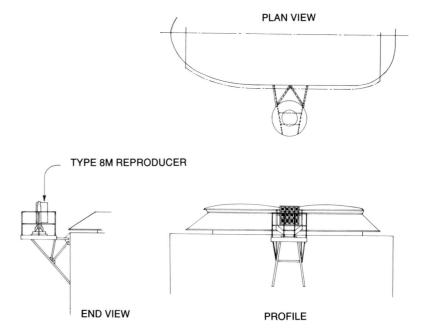

PLAN VIEW

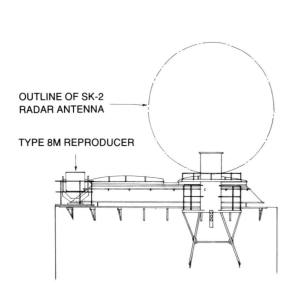

OUTLINE OF SK-2
RADAR ANTENNA

TYPE 8M REPRODUCER

TYPE 8M REPRODUCER

END VIEW

PROFILE

Details of the later style of SK platform as fitted to the *Franklin* and on the port side for the *Yorktown*.

Details of the platform to carry the Type 8M reproducer (loudspeaker); the precise position varied from ship to ship. A Type 8M was very often fitted at the aft end of the foremast radar platform.

1. Quadruple 40-mm
2. Mk 51 director
3. Mk 37 director
4. Mk 4 radar
5. Ensign gaff
6. SG radar platform
7. SC radar
8. Reproducer
9. YE homing beacon
10. SG radar
11. SK radar

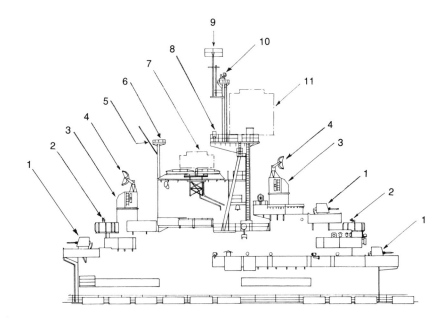

USS *Essex*—Island and Rig Configuration as Built in Early 1943

1. Quadruple 40-mm
2. Mk 49 director
3. Mk 51 director
4. Mk 37 director
5. Mk 12 radar
6. SK radar
7. SC radar
8. SG radar
9. YE homing beacon
10. SM radar

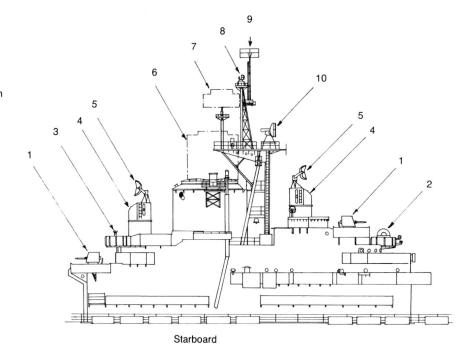

Starboard

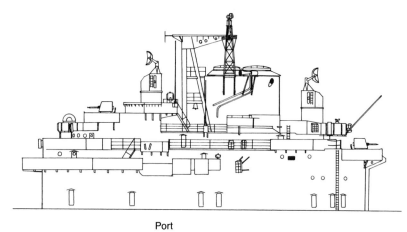

Port

USS *Essex*—Island and Rig Configuration as in April 1944

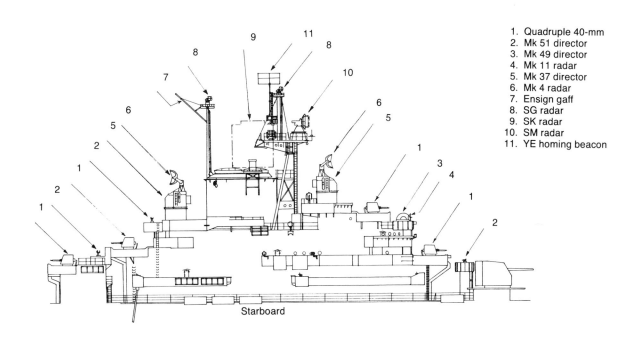

1. Quadruple 40-mm
2. Mk 51 director
3. Mk 49 director
4. Mk 11 radar
5. Mk 37 director
6. Mk 4 radar
7. Ensign gaff
8. SG radar
9. SK radar
10. SM radar
11. YE homing beacon

Starboard

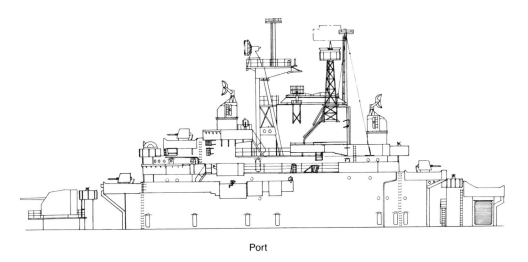

Port

USS *Lexington*—Island and Rig Configuration as in Late 1944

C. General Fittings and Equipment

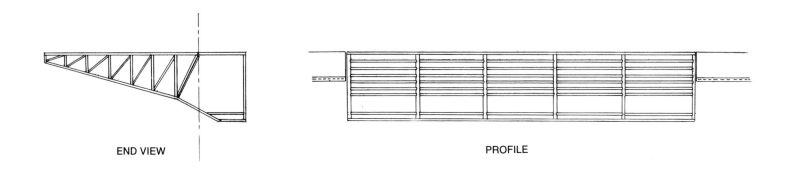

END VIEW

PROFILE

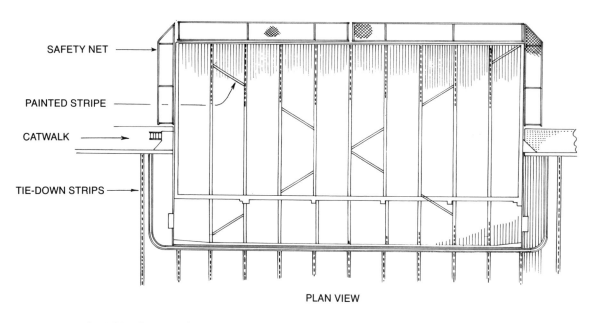

SAFETY NET

PAINTED STRIPE

CATWALK

TIE-DOWN STRIPS

PLAN VIEW

Deck Edge Elevator—General Arrangement Details

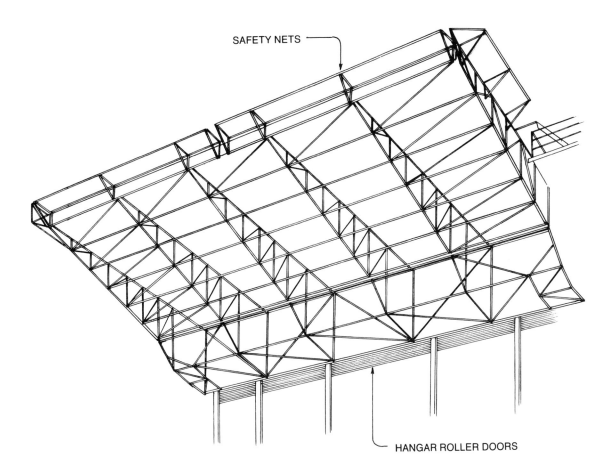

SAFETY NETS

HANGAR ROLLER DOORS

UNDERSIDE

Arrester Wires and Crash Barriers

Also shown are the tie-down metal strips spaced the length of the flight deck, and one of the bomb elevators; these were flush with the deck to allow free movement of the aircraft.

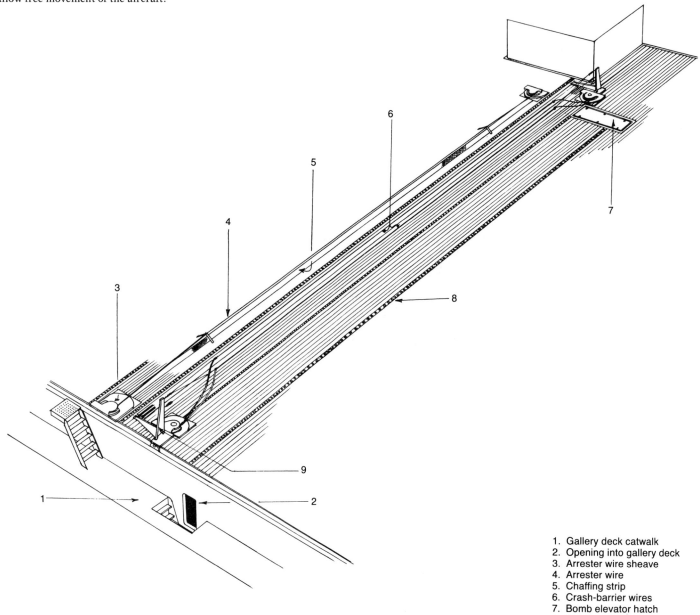

1. Gallery deck catwalk
2. Opening into gallery deck
3. Arrester wire sheave
4. Arrester wire
5. Chaffing strip
6. Crash-barrier wires
7. Bomb elevator hatch
8. Tie-down strip
9. Crash-barrier stanchion

1. Flight deck
2. Training gear box
3. Support girder
4. Training pinion
5. Paying-out gear

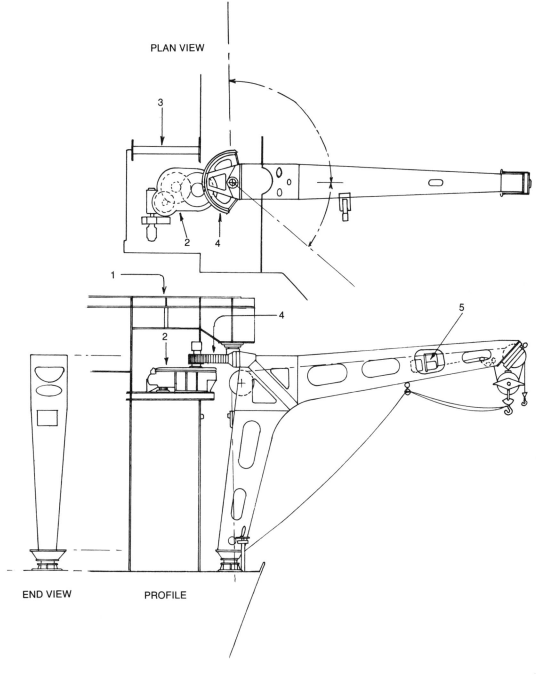

PLAN VIEW

END VIEW   PROFILE

Boat and Aircraft Crane

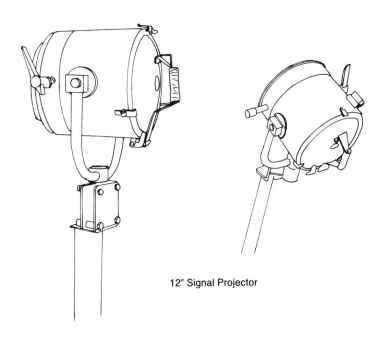

12″ Signal Projector

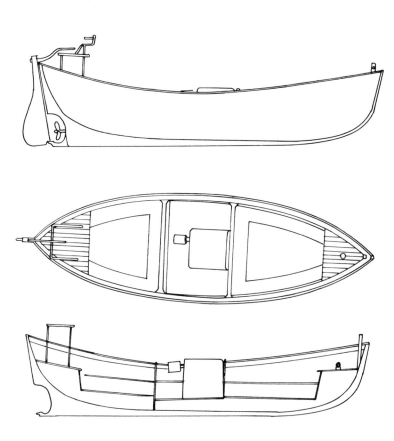

26′ Motor Whaleboat

The profile and plan view are for the wartime Mk 2, as are two of the perspective views, while the third perspective rendering is of the postwar all-plastic Mk 5.

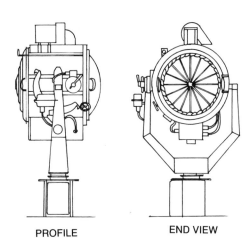

PROFILE   END VIEW

24″ Searchlight

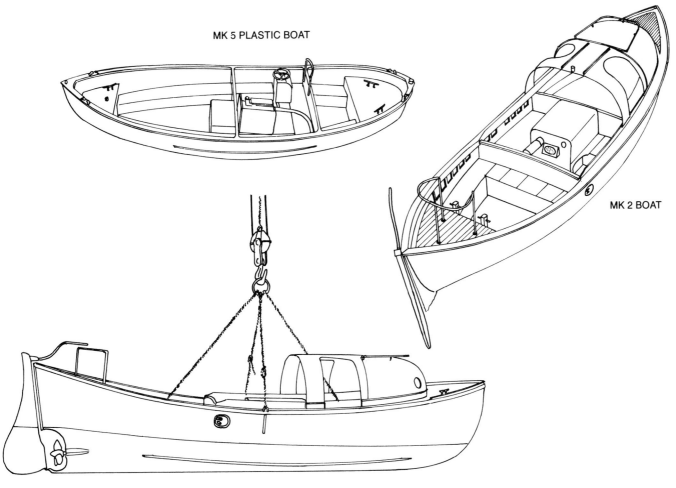

MK 5 PLASTIC BOAT

MK 2 BOAT

MK 2 BOAT

26' Motor Whaleboat

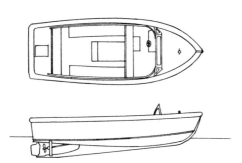

24′ Personnel Boat

As carried by the *Lexington* during the last months of the war. (See the general arrangement drawings for location.)

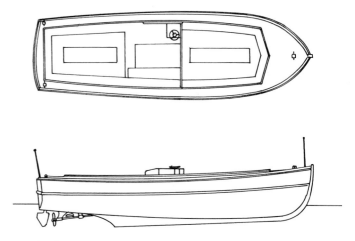

40′ Utility Boat

As carried by the *Antietam* in the late 1950s.

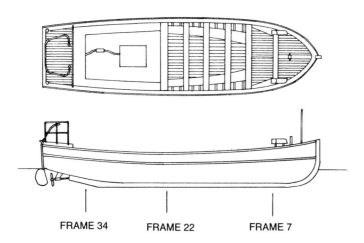

FRAME 34   FRAME 22   FRAME 7

40′ Motor Launch

Used for transporting large numbers of personnel, as carried on the *Kearsarge*.

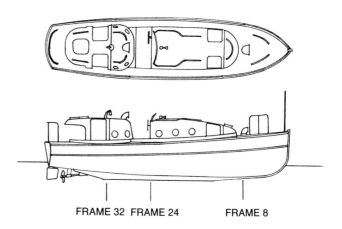

FRAME 32 FRAME 24   FRAME 8

35′ Motorboat

Used by officers on the *Kearsarge*.

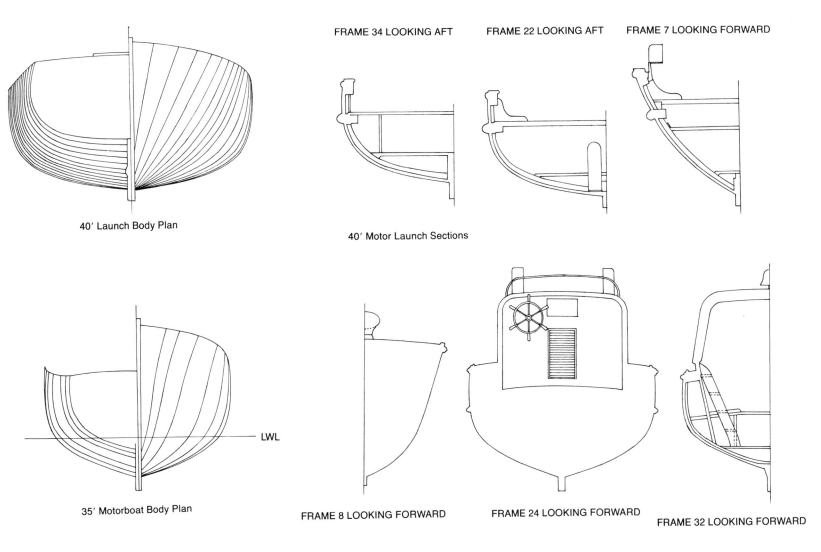

FRAME 34 LOOKING AFT   FRAME 22 LOOKING AFT   FRAME 7 LOOKING FORWARD

40′ Launch Body Plan

40′ Motor Launch Sections

LWL

35′ Motorboat Body Plan

FRAME 8 LOOKING FORWARD   FRAME 24 LOOKING FORWARD   FRAME 32 LOOKING FORWARD

35′ Motorboat Sections

D. Antennas

FRAMEWORK DIPOLES

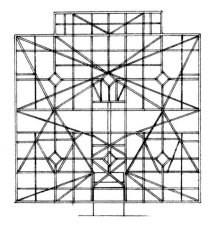

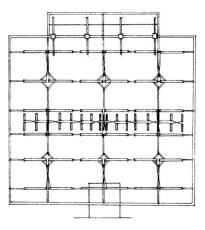

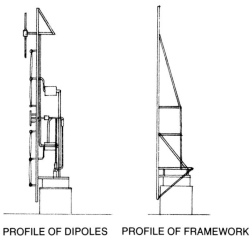

PROFILE OF DIPOLES   PROFILE OF FRAMEWORK

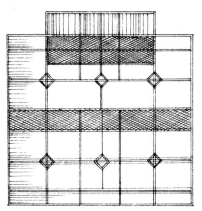

REFLECTING DIPOLES

Antenna Assembly for SK Air Search Radar

This was probably the most important radar set fitted to the *Essex* class in World War II. A long-range air search radar able to detect aircraft up to a distance of 100 nautical miles, it had a large 17-foot-by-17-foot antenna plus an IFF antenna attached along the top edge. Developed from the earlier SC, it was produced from January 1943, and the *Essex* was the first ship in the navy to be fitted with one. Initially positioned at the fore end of the foremast radar platform, it was later moved around to behind the foretopmast, or port or starboard of the funnel.

1. Parabolic reflector
2. IFF dipoles
3. Antenna framework
4. Wave guide
5. Mounting

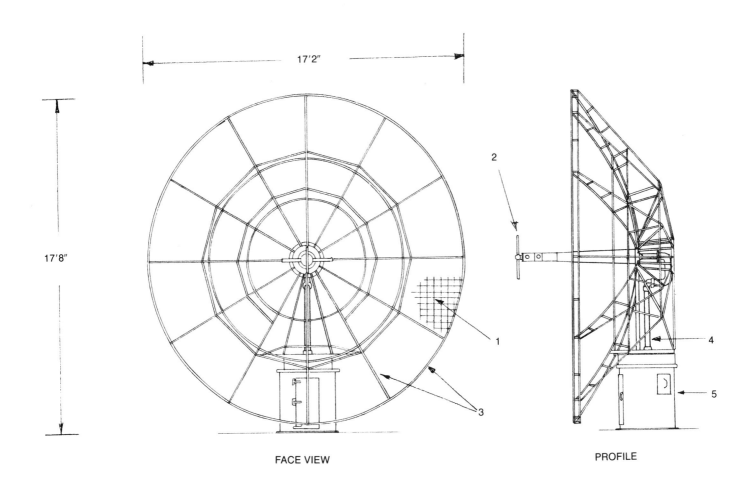

17'2"

17'8"

FACE VIEW

PROFILE

Antenna Assembly for SK-2 Air Search Radar

The SK-2 used a 17-foot dish antenna that dispensed with the unwanted side lobes produced by the square 17-foot-by-17-foot SK antenna. The SK-2 began to appear in late 1944, along with the introduction of the long-bow *Essex*es, and on those earlier units refitting from this time.

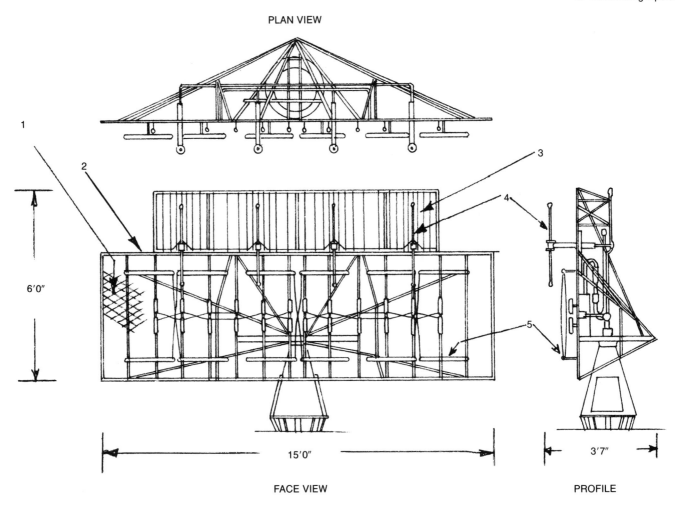

1. Reflector
2. Antenna framework
3. IFF reflecting dipoles
4. IFF transmitting dipoles
5. Transmitting dipoles

PLAN VIEW

FACE VIEW

PROFILE

6'0"

15'0"

3'7"

Antenna Assembly for SC-2, SC-3, and SC-4 Radar

This type of radar was fitted to all units except those completing at war's end and shortly thereafter. Antenna size was 15 feet by 4 feet 6 inches plus an IFF antenna carried along the top edge. SC was used as a backup to the more powerful SK or SK-2. It had a range of up to 80 nautical miles. SC-2, SC-3, and SC-4 used an identical antenna, and SC-2 could be upgraded to SC-3 and SC-4 standards. As with the SK, the location varied from the aft end of the foremast radar platform to either side of the funnel. As ships refitted in 1945, SC was replaced by the newer SR outfit.

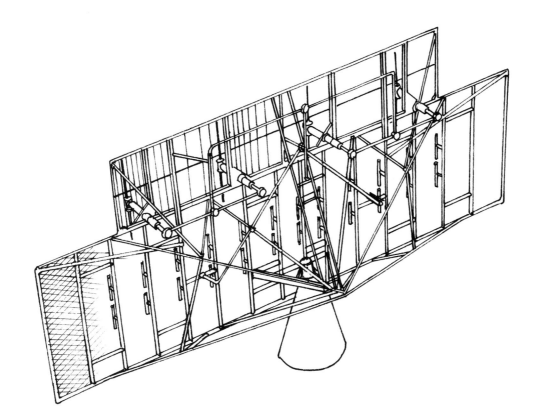

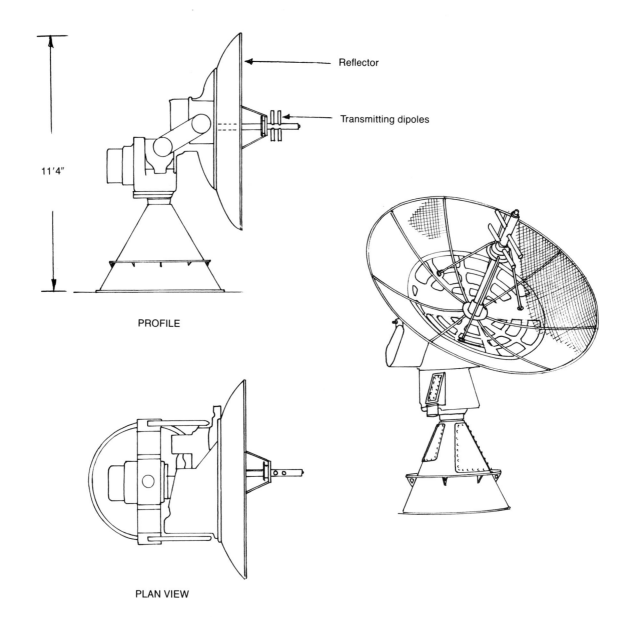

Reflector

Transmitting dipoles

11'4"

PROFILE

PLAN VIEW

Antenna Assembly for SP Radar

A lightweight successor to SM, SP began to appear in the first months of 1945. It used an 8-foot dish antenna and had a maximum range of 80 nautical miles. It was replaced in the postwar period by SX radar.

PLAN VIEW

Antenna Assembly for SR Radar

The first really new air search radar since type CXAM of 1940, it introduced a series of sets used for many years after the war. The main improvement over the SC series (which it replaced) was the provision of shock mountings for the equipment. Using a 15-foot-by-6-foot antenna, it had a maximum range of 110 nautical miles.

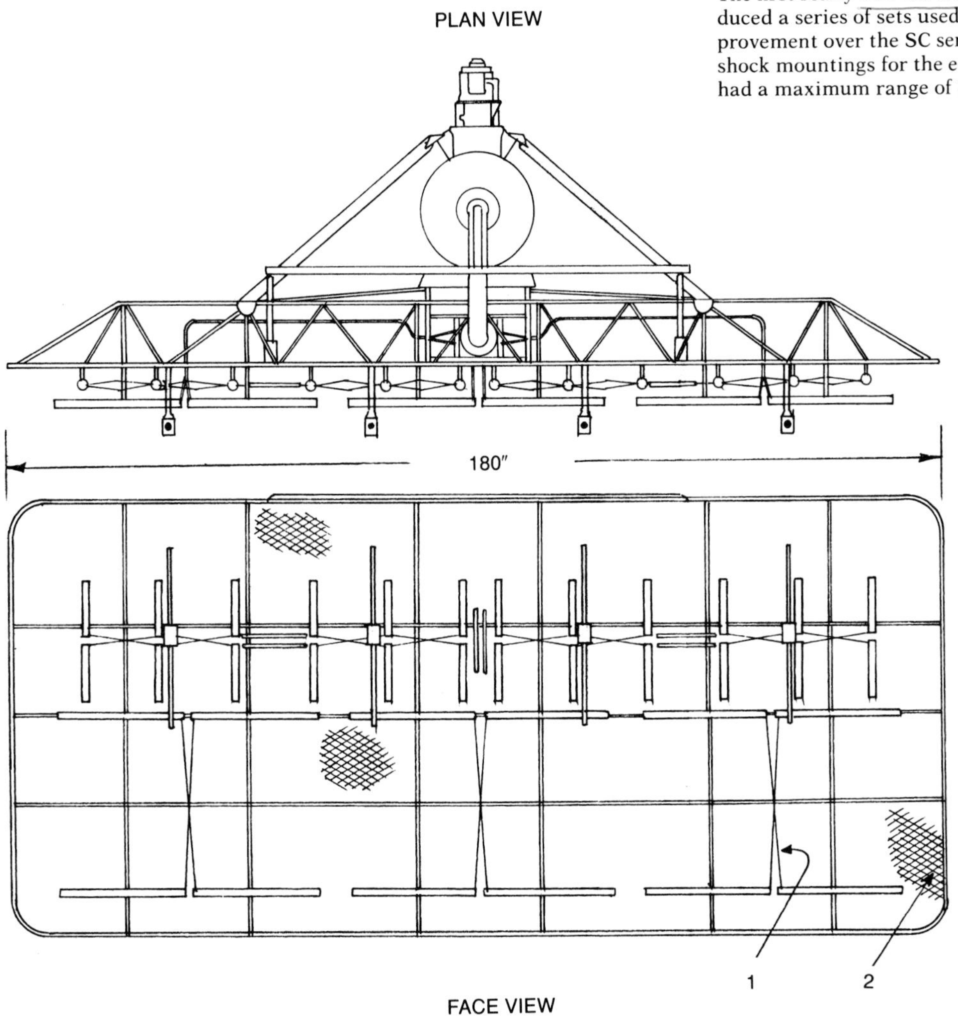

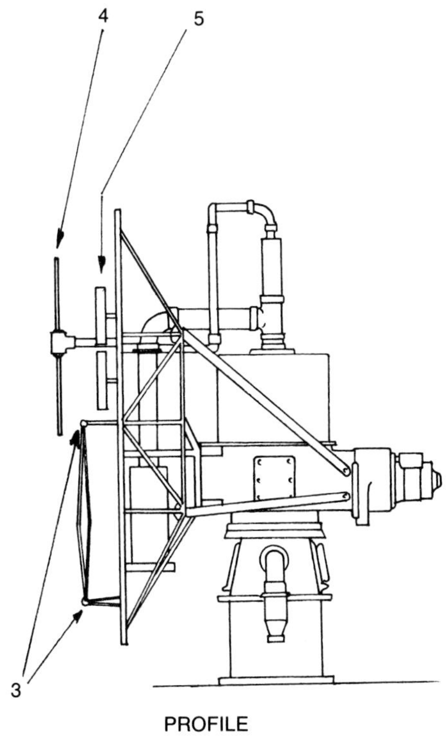

180"

FACE VIEW

PROFILE

1. Connecting wires
2. Reflector
3. Transmitting dipoles
4. IFF transmitting dipoles
5. IFF transmitting dipoles

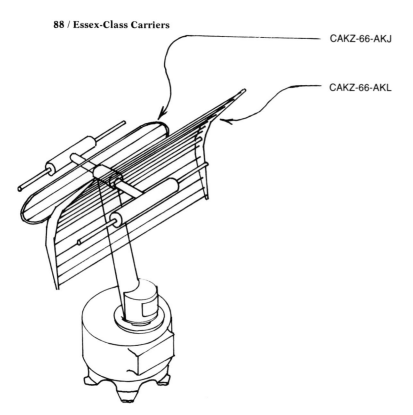

CAKZ-66-AKJ

CAKZ-66-AKL

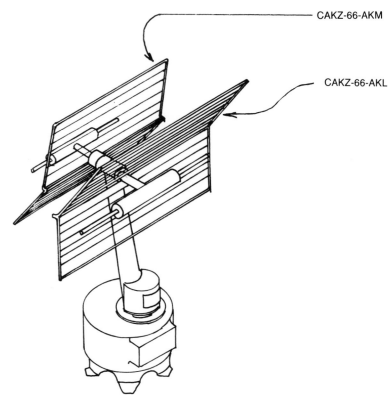

CAKZ-66-AKM

CAKZ-66-AKL

TDY Radar Jamming Antennas

As the Japanese began to use radar on a widespread basis in late 1944, the fleet introduced jammers on a large scale. Visually the most prominent were the sets that jammed in the shorter wavelengths. Types 66-AKL, 66-AKJ, and 66-AKM are shown here back to back to give the greatest coverage on a single mounting, usually installed on the port side of the funnel. Installations began in early 1945.

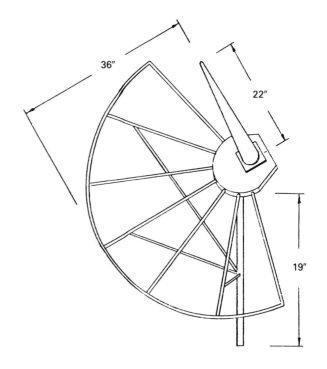

36"

22"

19"

Radar Intercept Antenna

An omnidirectional dipole antenna was used to pick up enemy radar transmissions. The fan-shaped rod arrangement is a ground plane and not part of the antenna proper. The antennas were fitted in pairs, usually to the sides of the funnel.

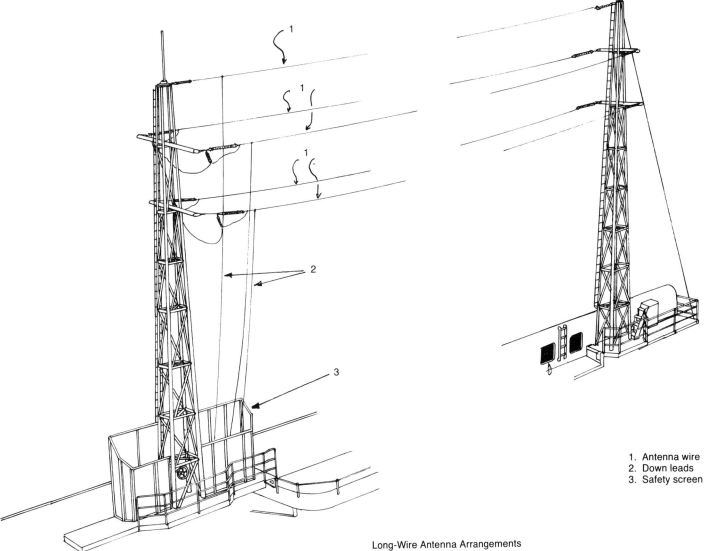

1. Antenna wire
2. Down leads
3. Safety screen

Long-Wire Antenna Arrangements

These were fitted to every *Essex* as built (with the sole exception of the late-completing *Oriskany*). The sets were arranged fore and aft of the island along the starboard edge of the flight deck. Small details of the outrigger arrangements sometimes varied between ships. The drawing shows the *Leyte*'s rig as built.

E. Weapons and Associated Equipment

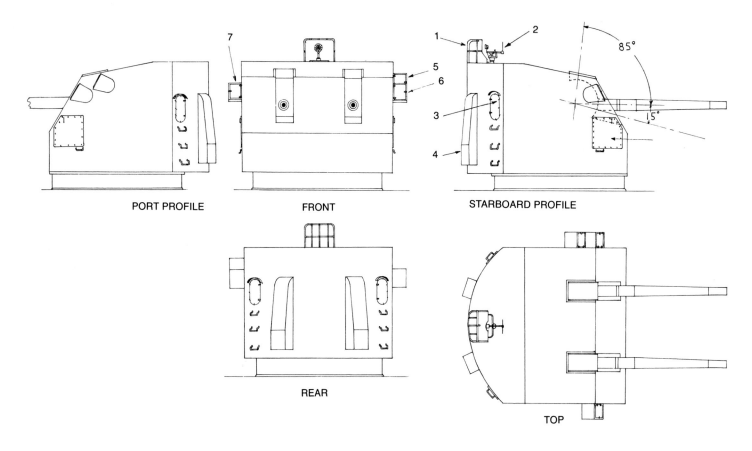

PORT PROFILE

FRONT

STARBOARD PROFILE

85°

5°

REAR

TOP

Twin 5" Mounting

1. Blast hood
2. Gunsight for use when the mounting is in local control
3. Access door
4. Disposal chute for used shells
5. Checker's telescope
6. Pointer's telescope
7. Trainer's telescope

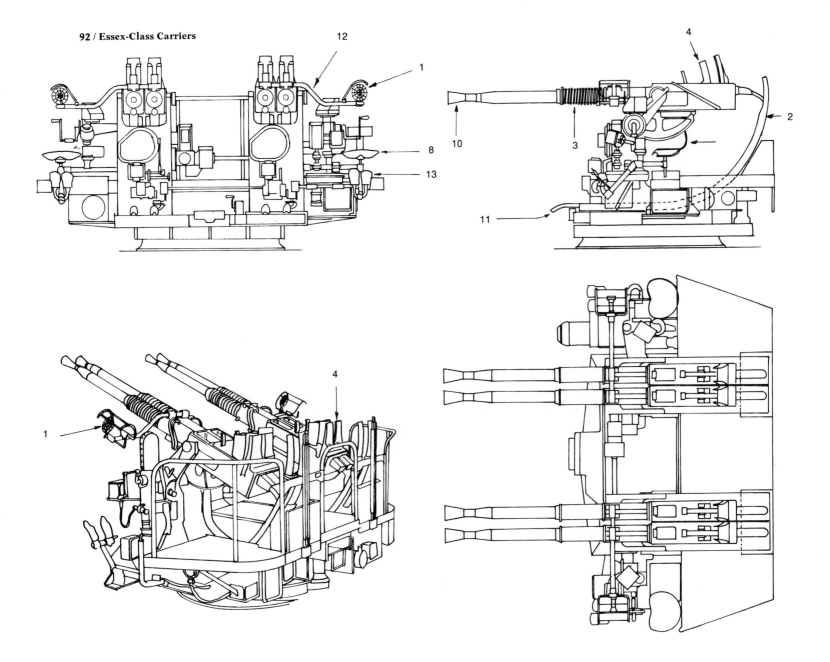

Quadruple 40-mm Mk 4 Mounting

This mounting was fitted in substantial numbers to every vessel as built. The gun design was of Swedish origin, and was water-cooled as opposed to the air-cooled guns used in single "army" mountings. Each gun was loaded from the top of the breach by clips of four shells. The rate of fire was 160 rounds per minute per barrel, with an effective range of 2500 yards. In the first vessels of the *Essex* class to complete in early 1943, the fit was eight mounts. This was increased as the war progressed, so that by the war's end up to seventeen were on the short-bow ships and eighteen on the long-bow ships.

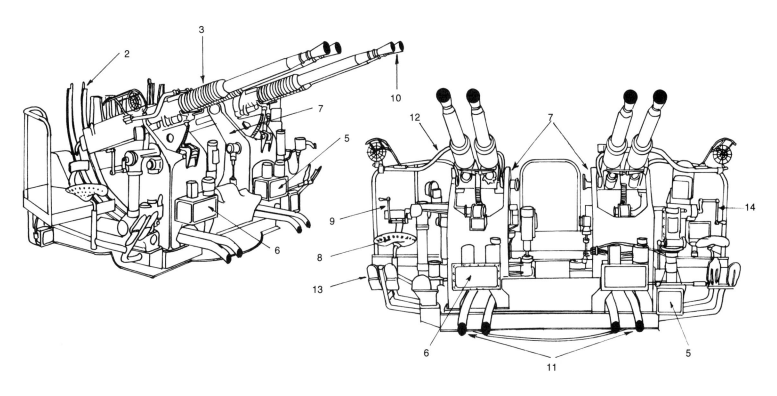

1. Sight
2. Used-shell chute
3. Recoil springs
4. Loading position
5. Elevation power drive
6. Training power drive
7. Carriage
8. Seat
9. Training crank
10. Flash guard
11. Used-shell discharge chutes
12. Sight bar
13. Footrest (starboard) and firing pedal (port)
14. Elevating crank

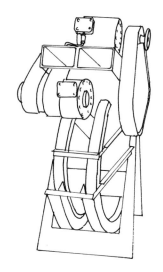

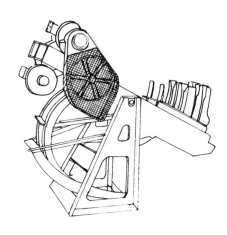

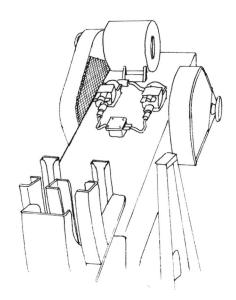

40-mm Practice Loader

To assist in the operation of the 40-mm mountings, several vessels, including the *Lexington*, were fitted with a practice loader by the war's end.

1. Fore sight
2. Back sight
3. Magazine drum
4. Splinter shield
5. Shoulder rests
6. Used-shell bag
7. Mounting
8. Pedestal-elevating handwheel

Twin 20-mm Oerlikon Mounting

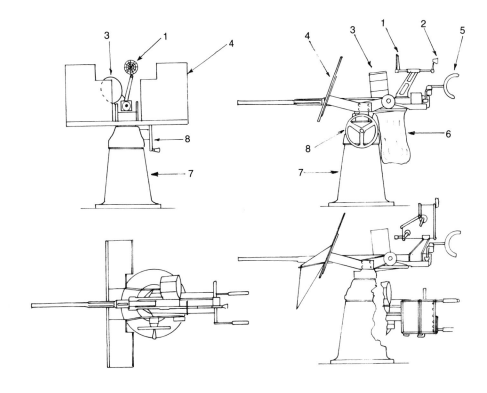

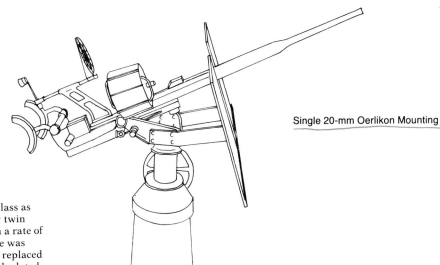

Single 20-mm Oerlikon Mounting

The ubiquitous 20-mm gun was fitted in large numbers to the class as built. The single mounting began to be replaced in late 1944 by twin mountings. A hand-worked gun, it fired a 0.27-pound shell with a rate of fire of 450 rounds per minute per gun. Maximum effective range was 1,000 yards. In late 1943 the original ring gunsight began to be replaced by the Mk 14 lead computing gunsight, which automatically calculated the degree of aim-off required.

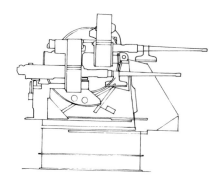

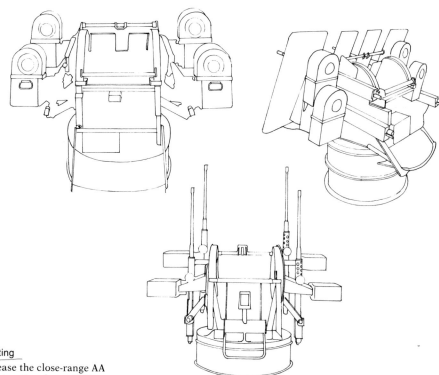

Army Type M45 0.5″ Quadruple Machine Gun Mounting

This was introduced as a means of trying to increase the close-range AA capability to combat the kamikaze. Capable of saturation fire at 2800 rounds per barrel per minute, it took up the same deck area as did the twin 20-mm. Six of these mountings were fitted to the *Lexington* and *Wasp* in the spring of 1945.

F. Fire-Control Equipment

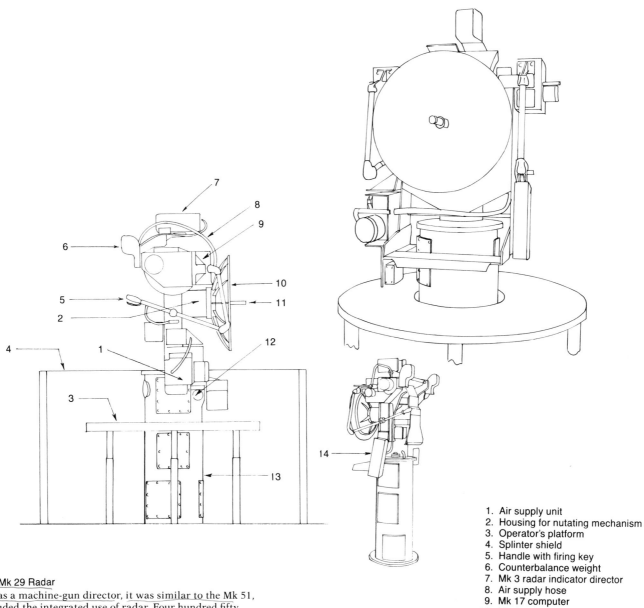

Mk 57 Director with Mk 29 Radar

Developed in 1943 as a machine-gun director, it was similar to the Mk 51, but the design included the integrated use of radar. Four hundred fifty were ordered, and deliveries to the fleet began in late 1944. As the *Essex* class refitted in late 1944 and early 1945, there was a replacement of some of their Mk 51 directors by Mk 57s, so that by the war's end there was a scattering of Mk 57s in use on most of the class.

1. Air supply unit
2. Housing for nutating mechanism
3. Operator's platform
4. Splinter shield
5. Handle with firing key
6. Counterbalance weight
7. Mk 3 radar indicator director
8. Air supply hose
9. Mk 17 computer
10. Mk 4 radar antenna
11. Antenna feed
12. Range potentiometer
13. Mounting
14. Mk 5 power supply

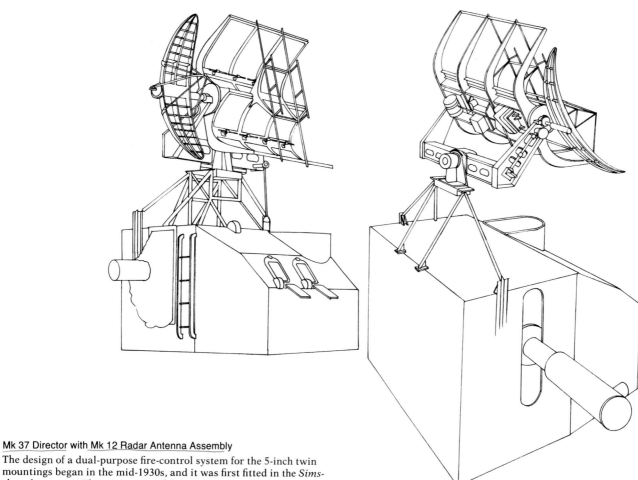

Mk 37 Director with Mk 12 Radar Antenna Assembly

The design of a dual-purpose fire-control system for the 5-inch twin mountings began in the mid-1930s, and it was first fitted in the *Sims*-class destroyers. This very successful director was used throughout the wartime fleet and was able to handle all forms of air attack up until the introduction of the Japanese kamikaze *Baka* bombs in 1945. Fitted with the Mk 4 radar with its twin parabolic trough antennas carried on the roof of the director, it became the premier dual-purpose director of the war years. Its only drawback was the inability to attain blind fire; hence the introduction of the Mk 12 radar that used the same antenna. At the same time that the Mk 12 was introduced, so was the associated height-finder set (Mk 22) that used a small cut parabolic antenna set vertically and attached to one side of the Mk 4 or Mk 12 antenna. Every early *Essex* completed with the Mk 4, and the later ones with the Mk 12/22. The Mk 4 could be converted to Mk 12, and many underwent this change in 1944.

1. Reflector for Mk 12 radar antenna
2. Reflector for IFF antenna
3. IFF transmitting dipoles
4. Cross-level connecting rod to radar antenna
5. Captain's observation position
6. 15′ rangefinder
7. Bracing strut
8. Reflector bracing
9. Mk 22 antenna attachment point
10. Transmitting equipment for Mk 22 radar attachment
11. Cradle for antenna assembly

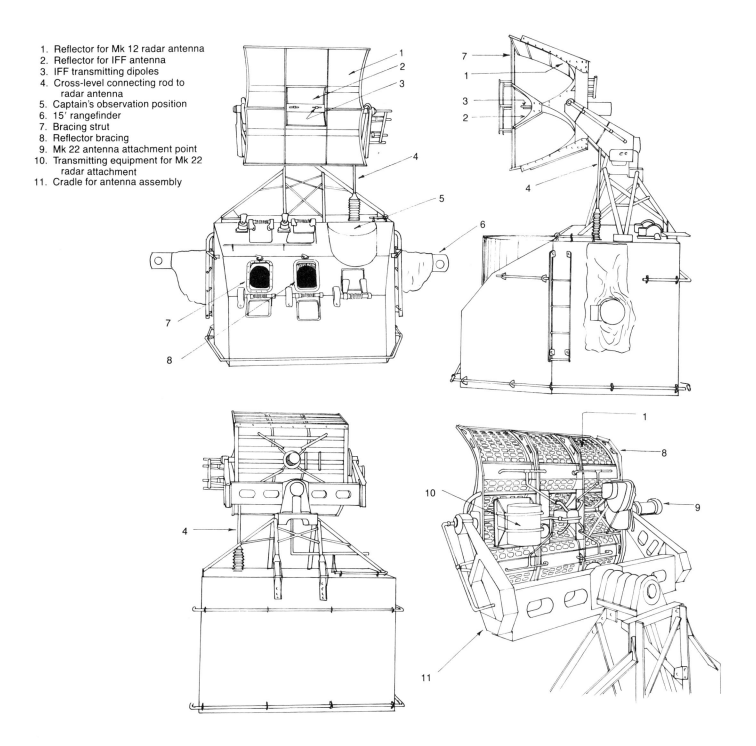

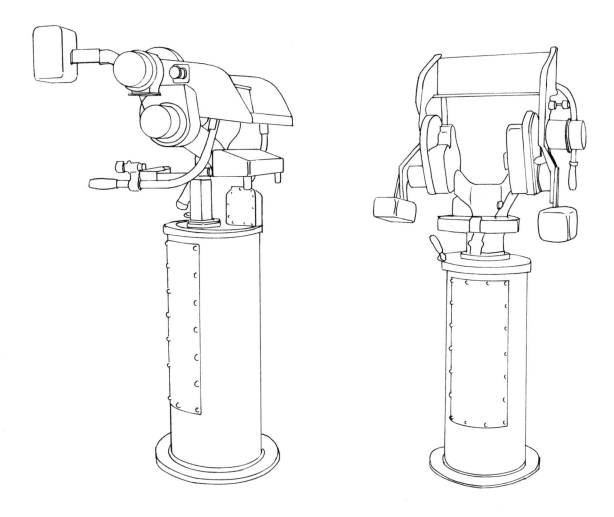

Mk 51 Director

This was a manually operated, lightweight piece of equipment, in essence a simple mount with a Mk 14 gunsight attached. It was used to control the 40-mm mountings, and as these increased in number so did the Mk 51 directors.

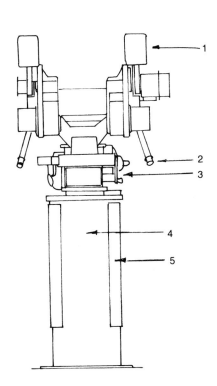

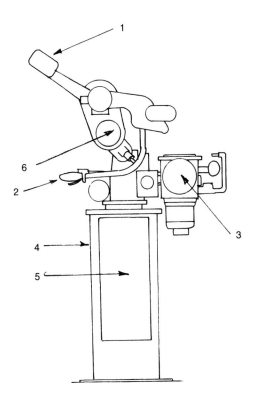

1. Counterbalance weights
2. Handle and firing key
3. Motor
4. Mounting
5. Access plate
6. Elevation synchro unit

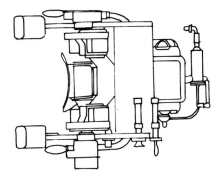

G. Camouflage, 1944

USS *Essex*

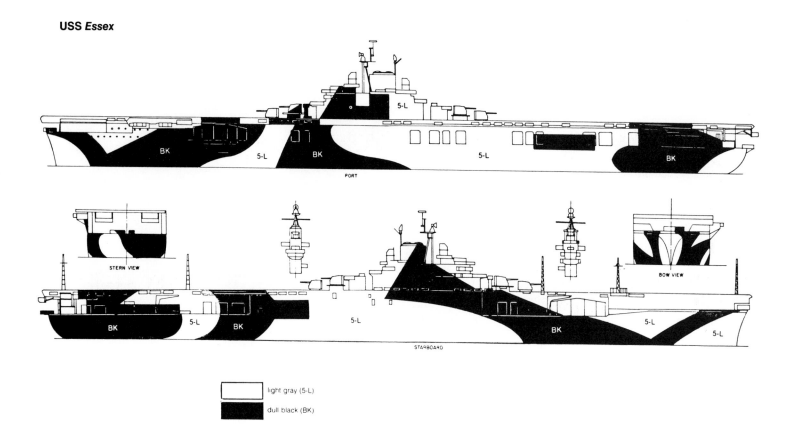

light gray (5-L)

dull black (BK)

The flight decks were painted with a blue stain called #21 blue flight
deck stain. Flight deck numbers were almost always black, but occasion-
ally reported by late in the war as being a dark blue (20b deck blue). The
broken guidelines that ran fore and aft along the flight deck were yellow
or light gray, and then white very late in the war. Similarly painted were
the Xs across the elevators and around their edges.

USS *Hornet*

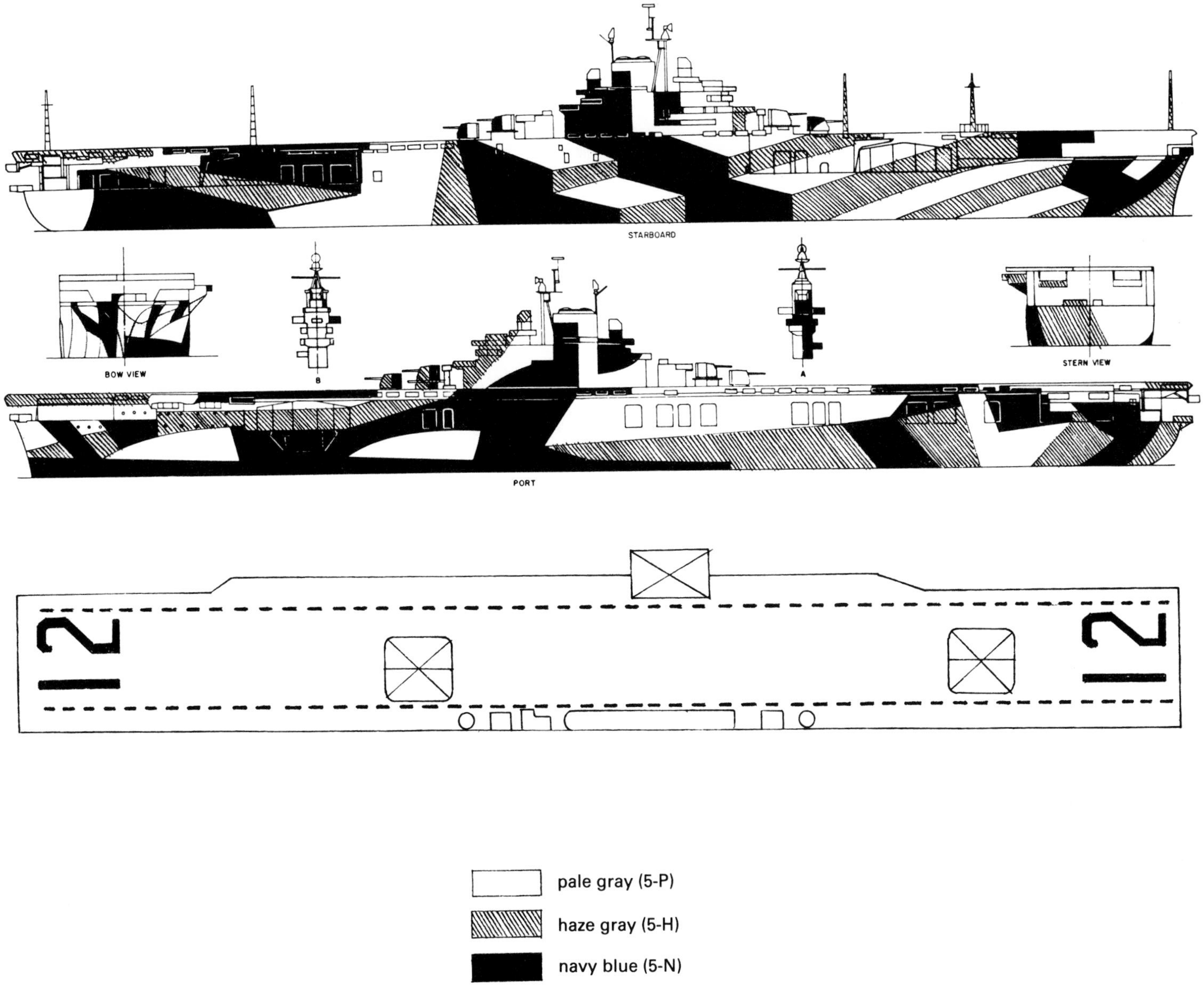
STARBOARD
BOW VIEW
B
A
STERN VIEW
PORT
12
12
pale gray (5-P)
haze gray (5-H)
navy blue (5-N)

USS *Ticonderoga*

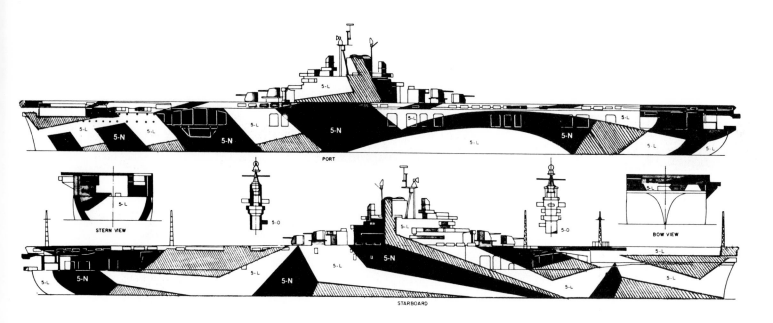

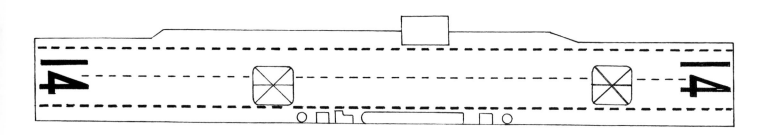

light gray (5-L)
ocean gray (5-O)
navy blue (5-N)

USS *Bennington*

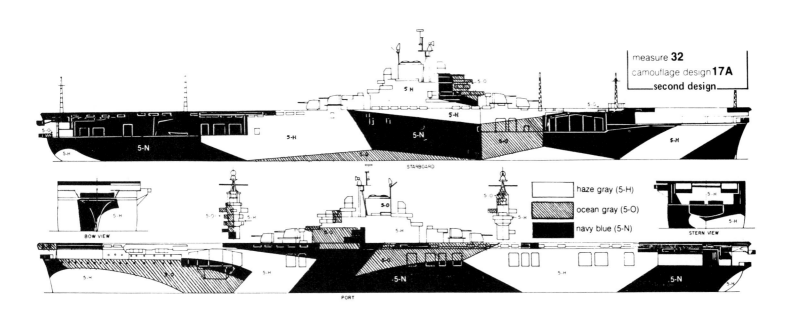

measure **32**
camouflage design **17A**
second design

STARBOARD

BOW VIEW

PORT

STERN VIEW

	haze gray (5-H)
	ocean gray (5-O)
	navy blue (5-N)

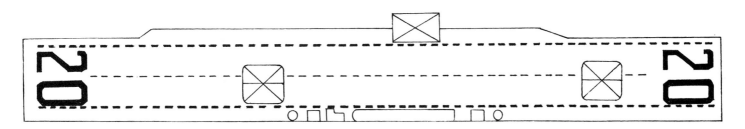

	haze gray (5-H)
	ocean gray (5-O)
	navy blue (5-N)

H. Combat Damage

USS *Franklin*—Bomb Damage, 19 March 1945

Hangar Deck Showing Position of Aircraft

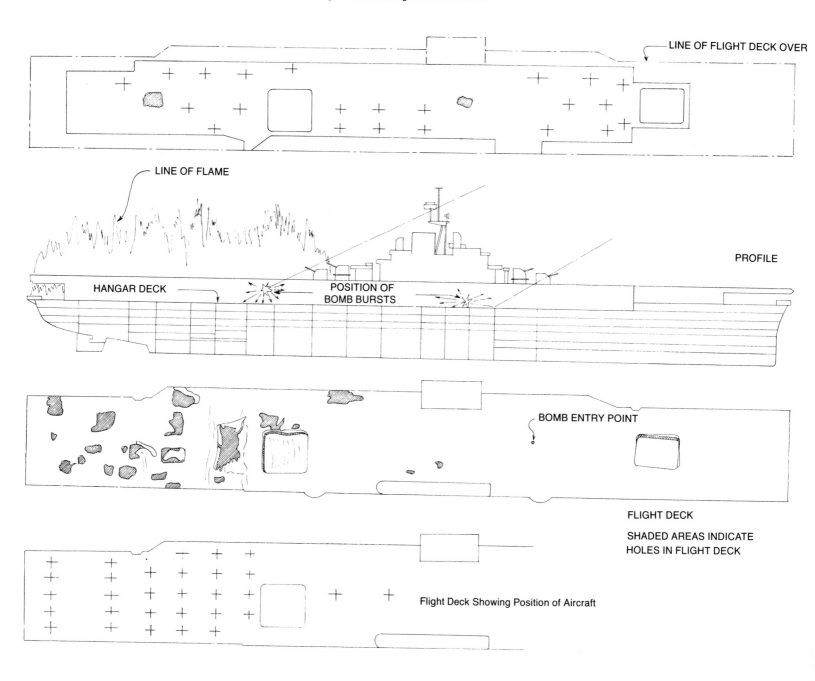

LINE OF FLIGHT DECK OVER

LINE OF FLAME

PROFILE

HANGAR DECK

POSITION OF
BOMB BURSTS

BOMB ENTRY POINT

FLIGHT DECK

SHADED AREAS INDICATE
HOLES IN FLIGHT DECK

Flight Deck Showing Position of Aircraft

There were two occasions when damage to an *Essex* threatened to sink the ship. One was the *Franklin:* she was hit by two bombs that penetrated the flight deck, causing extensive damage, fires, and flooding. The extent of the damage necessitated a complete rebuilding of the ship from hangar deck level upward, the only exception being the island structure.

Postwar Photographs

The stern of the *Princeton* at Philadelphia on 10 April 1946, soon after
completion. Of interest is the line of whip antennas laid along the edge of
the gallery deck. Like the old-style lattice masts that carried the long
wire antennas, these new antennas could be swung from the vertical to
the horizontal position to allow flight deck operations to take place. The
six teardrop-shaped objects facing the camera are smoke-dispensing can-
isters.

Midship view of the *Princeton* during her final fitting-out at the Philadelphia yard in December 1945. The elimination of the very long internal vent trunk on the second deck is shown by the presence of new outboard venting arrangements just below the gallery deck platforms, seen here as prominent bulges.

The *Leyte* fitting out at Newport News in March 1946. This picture was
taken during her inclining experiment.

The *Leyte* completed and in service, showing the new SX radar on the fore-mast platform. The radome on the fore side of the topmast contains the antenna for the zenith search SCR-720 radar. This was an air force set used in night fighters but adapted for shipboard use; it was replaced by SG-6 or SG-6b beginning in mid-1945. (National Archives)

One of the last of the class to complete was the *Philippine Sea*, seen here entering San Francisco in 1952 after her second Korean tour.

To test the use of the angled deck before large-scale application to the fleet, the *Antietam* was taken in hand in 1952 to have her flight deck extended accordingly. The photo shows her as she appeared in 1954 before a further refit in which her rig was changed (see the general arrangement plans).

Heavy weather was no deterrent to operations, as this picture of the *Essex* shows. This view dates from late 1959. (Official U.S. Navy photograph)

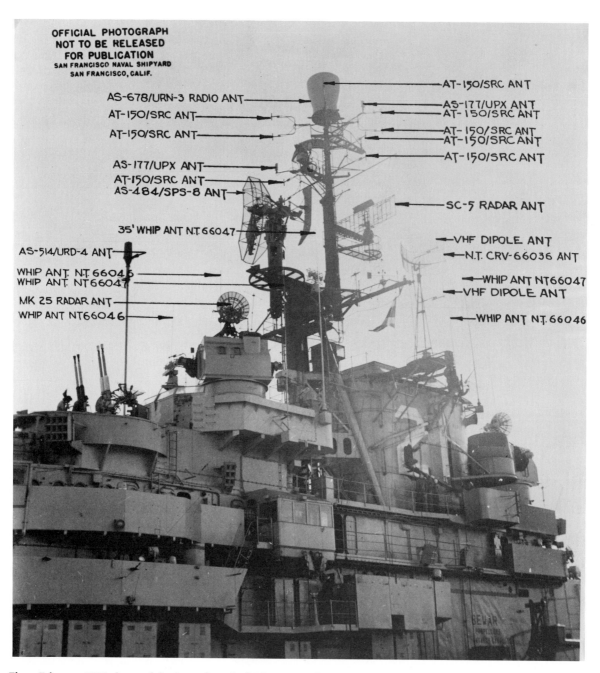

AS-678/URN-3 RADIO ANT

AT-150/SRC ANT

AT-150/SRC ANT

AS-177/UPX ANT

AT-150/SRC ANT
AS-484/SPS-8 ANT

35' WHIP ANT N.T. 66047

AS-514/URD-4 ANT

WHIP ANT. N.T. 66046
WHIP ANT. NT 66047

MK 25 RADAR ANT

WHIP ANT NT 66046

AT-150/SRC ANT

AS-177/UPX ANT
AT-150/SRC ANT

AT-150/SRC ANT
AT-150/SRC ANT

AT-150/SRC ANT

SC-5 RADAR ANT

VHF DIPOLE ANT

N.T. CRV-66036 ANT

WHIP ANT NT66047
VHF DIPOLE ANT

WHIP ANT N.T. 66046

These February 1955 photos of the *Boxer* show the fairly minor refitting
that was given to the unconverted ships still in service. It was mostly
given over to an upgrading of communications, as seen by the large number of tilting whips along the deck edge and around the island.

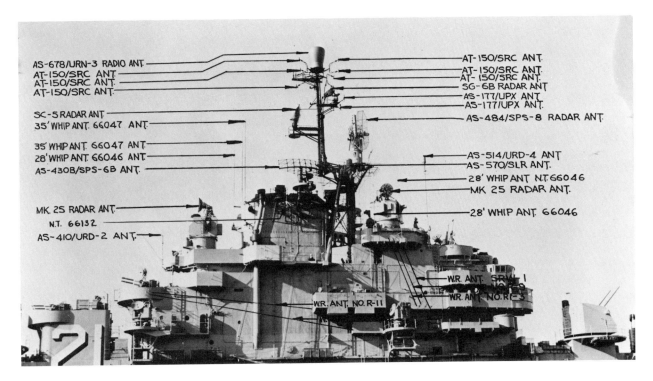

AS-678/URN-3 RADIO ANT.
AT-150/SRC ANT.
AT-150/SRC ANT.
AT-150/SRC ANT.

AT-150/SRC ANT.
AT-150/SRC ANT.
AT-150/SRC ANT.
SG-6B RADAR ANT.
AS-177/UPX ANT.
AS-177/UPX ANT.
AS-484/SPS-8 RADAR ANT.

SC-5 RADAR ANT.
35' WHIP ANT. 66047 ANT.

35' WHIP ANT. 66047 ANT.
28' WHIP ANT. 66046 ANT.
AS-430B/SPS-6B ANT.

AS-514/URD-4 ANT
AS-570/SLR ANT.
28' WHIP ANT. N.T. 66046
MK 25 RADAR ANT.

MK. 25 RADAR ANT.
N.T. 66132
AS-410/URD-2 ANT.

28' WHIP ANT. 66046

W.R. ANT. SRW. 1
W.R. ANT. NO. RC-3

W.R. ANT. NO. R-11

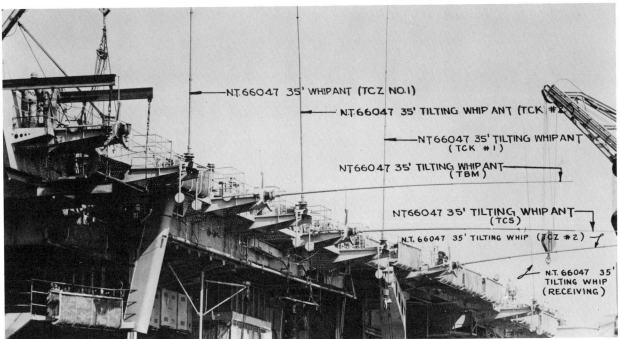

N.T. 66047 35' WHIP ANT. (TCZ NO.1)

N.T. 66047 35' TILTING WHIP ANT (TCK #2)

NT 66047 35' TILTING WHIP ANT.
(TCK #1)

NT 66047 35' TILTING WHIP ANT.
(TBM)

NT 66047 35' TILTING WHIP ANT.
(TCS)

N.T. 66047 35' TILTING WHIP (TCZ #2)

N.T. 66047 35'
TILTING WHIP
(RECEIVING)

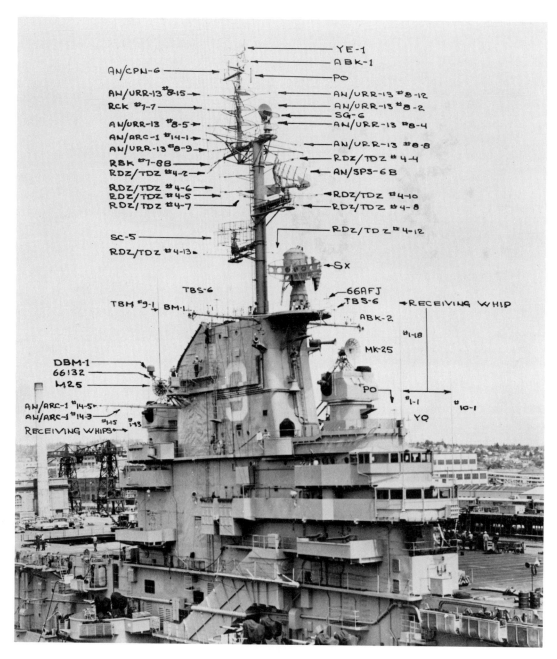

A close-up of the island of the *Essex* in June 1952 at the end of a yard
period at Puget Sound, typical of the early conversions with modern sensors and communications. Of special interest is the combined surface
search and zenith search antenna for the SG-6 radar.

The *Essex*, seen here after her 1955/56 SCB-125 conversion. (Official U.S. Navy photograph)

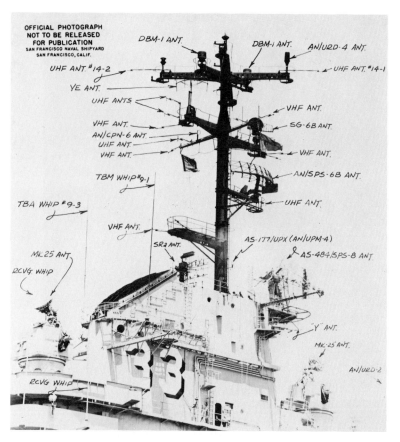

The island of the *Kearsarge* in January 1954. Of interest is the installation of the SRa radar. It was originally planned to fit paired SPS-6b radars for complete air search coverage, but as production was not able to meet this requirement, the second outfit became SR, which happened to have a detection range of 100 nautical miles as opposed to about 80 for the SPS-6b.

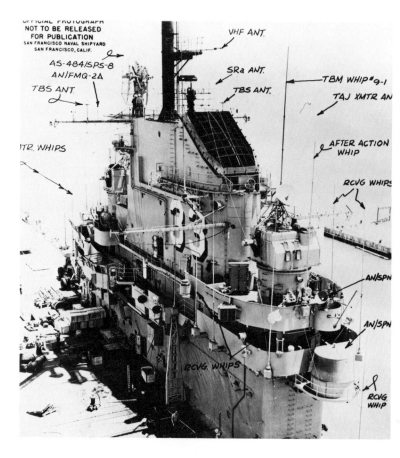

The *Kearsarge* long after her SCB-125 conversion. The most important difference in respect of rig is the fitting of the very large antenna for the SPS-43a radar, slung outboard from the funnel top platform. (Official U.S. Navy photograph)

The *Intrepid* as she appeared in 1955 in her SCB-27c configuration. The 40-mm quadruple mounts have been removed, as have the twin 5-inch mounts by the island. Her AA capability consists primarily of twin automatic 3-inch mounts ranged down the port and starboard sides.

Two views of the automatic twin 3-inch mount. This weapon was the result of a search for a replacement for the 40-mm. The new gun began to appear in 1948 and was fitted to all *Essex*es that underwent conversion. It had a rate of fire of forty to fifty rounds per minute and was controlled by the Mk 56 director coupled with the Mk 35 radar.

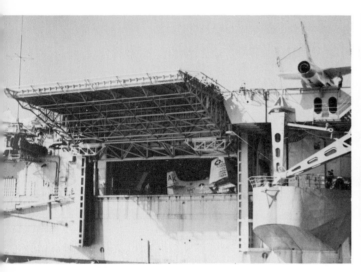

Looking along the starboard side of the *Intrepid*, operating off Vietnam in the 1960s.

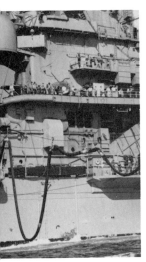

Rear and front angles of the Mk 56 director that was used to control the twin 3-inch mounts fitted in the *Essex* class after the war. For blind fire capability, the director was coupled with the Mk 35 radar, the dish antenna for which was attached to the port side of the cockpit.

Bow view of the *Intrepid* as she appeared in the late 1960s in almost her final configuration.

Two close-ups of the bridge of the *Intrepid* taken in 1972, showing her last appearance before decommissioning. The radar jamming antennas are fitted on the end of outriggers extending from the box attached high up on the starboard side of the island. U.S. Navy markings on the photographs identify the antennas. (Official U.S. Navy photographs)

Looking up the mast of the *Intrepid*. For details of the various antennas, refer to the drawings.

The end—the *Oriskany* being laid up in reserve in September 1976. At the time of writing, the ship is still laid up at Bremerton, Washington, with her sisters the *Hornet, Bennington,* and *Bon Homme Richard.* (Official U.S. Navy photograph)

Postwar Drawings

A. General Arrangement Plans

General arrangement plans of the USS *Kearsarge* as she appeared in July 1954 in her SCB-27a conversion. The 40-mm quadruple mounts have been removed and replaced with fourteen twin 3-inch mountings. The island has been completely remodeled, the twin 5-inch mounts removed, and a completely new rig with a heavy pole mast has replaced the old tripod type. Radars carried are SPS-8, SPS-6a, SPS-4, SR, SPN-6, SPN-8, and SPN-12. Mk 25s replace the Mk 12s on the Mk 37 directors, and the 3-inch mounts have the Mk 56 director with Mk 35 radar. The mast is capped by the Tactical Aid to Navigation beacon (TACAN), and on the platform immediately below are antennas for communications, direction-finding, and jamming. The flight deck shows larger elevators fore and at the deck edge, and the more powerful H8 catapults. To reduce the wear on the landing area aft caused by the heavier aircraft (including jets) used at this time, a 25-pound special treatment steel plate has been let into the flight deck.

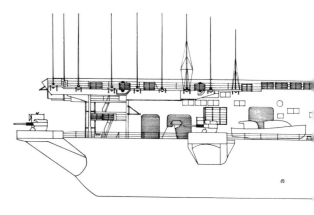

USS *Kearsarge*—Starboard Outboard Profile

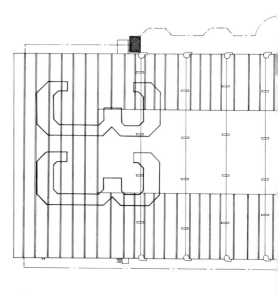

USS *Kearsarge*—Flight Deck

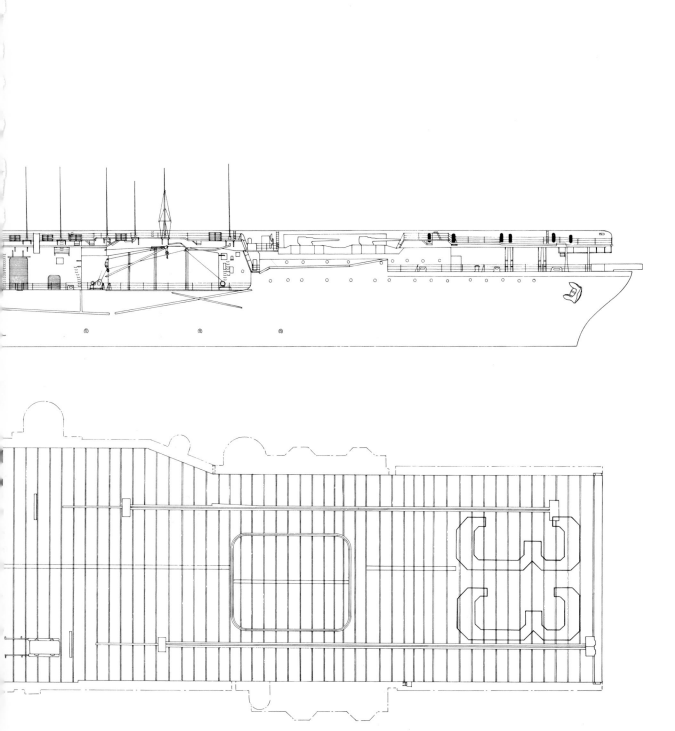

USS *Kearsarge*—Port Outboard Profile

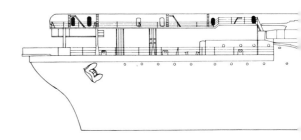

Key to Gallery Deck

1. Secondary conning station
2. Crew's berthing
3. Gas station
4. Elevator trunk
5. Mk 56 director radar room
6. 5" handling room
7. Electronics workshop
8. Radio transmitter room
9. Officer's WC
10. Junior officers' bunk room
11. Bomb elevator
12. Admiral's cabin
13. Captain's cabin
14. Captain's stateroom
15. Captain's pantry
16. Emergency dressing station
17. Staff office
18. Staff officer's stateroom
19. CIC
20. Squadron ready room
21. Air combat intelligence
22. Flag office
23. Radio countermeasures room
24. Air operations
25. Carrier-controlled approach (CCA) control room
26. Operations department office
27. Air department office
28. Main communications office
29. Radio central
30. Uptakes
31. Aviation repair shop
32. Squadron armory
33. Electronics repair shop
34. Aviation bomb director shop
35. Squadron office
36. Parachute packing space
37. Aircraft ammunition belting room
38. Control surface stowage
39. Whip antenna

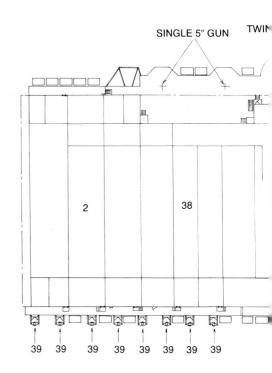

SINGLE 5" GUN   TWIN

USS *Kearsarge*—Gallery Deck

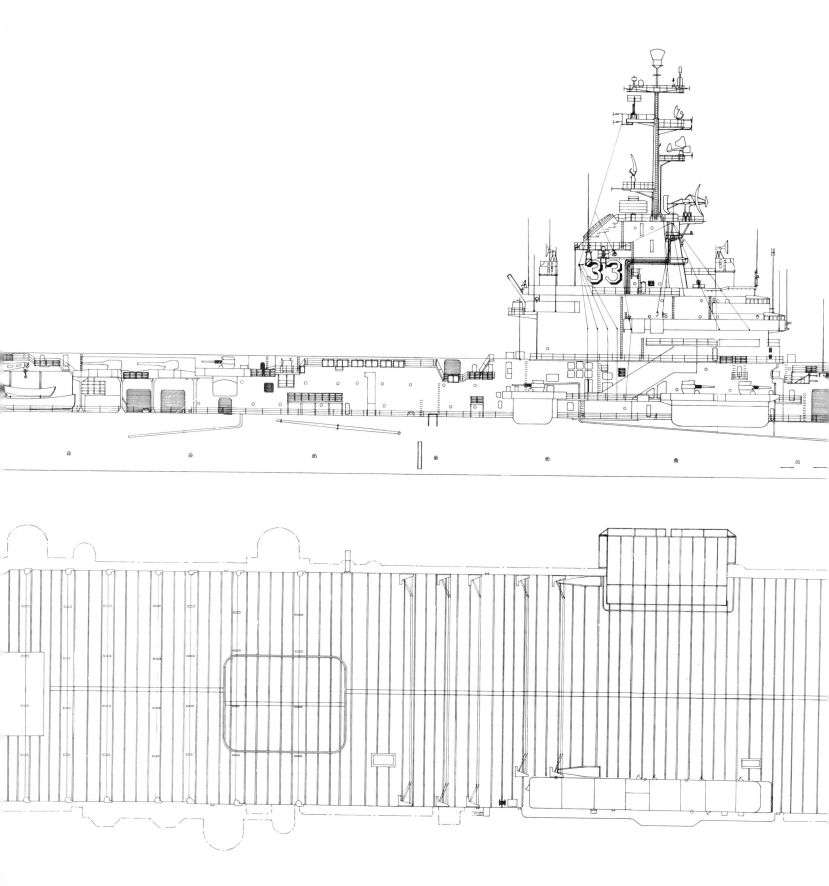

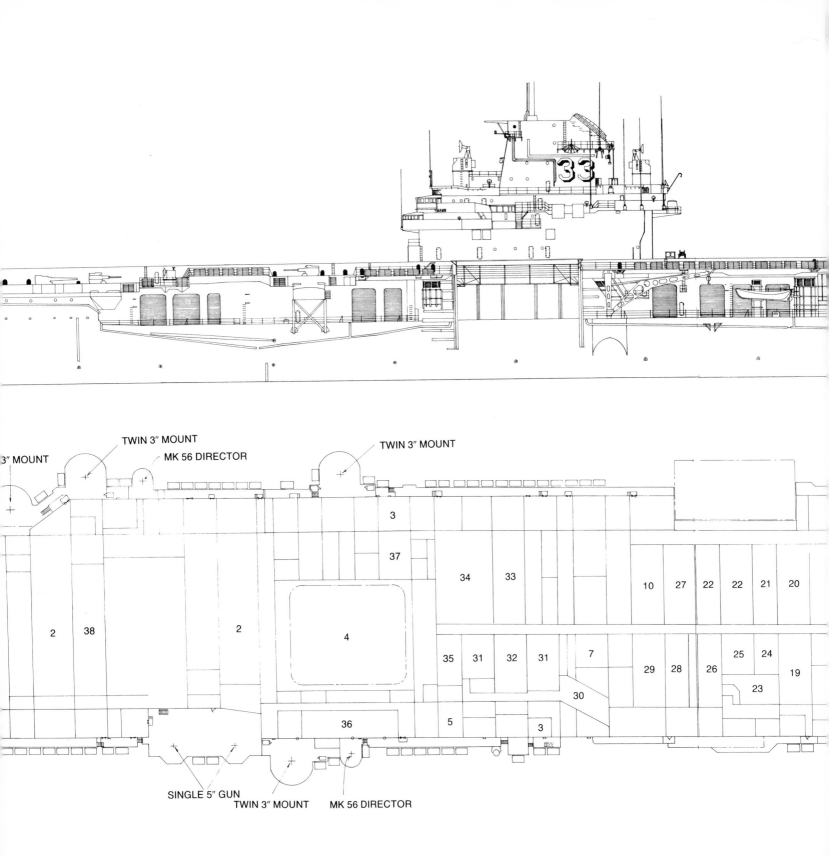

TWIN 3″ MOUNT

MK 56 DIRECTOR

3″ MOUNT

TWIN 3″ MOUNT

3

37

34   33

10   27   22   22   21   20

2   38

2

4

35   31   32   31   7

25   24

29   28   26

23

19

30

36

5

3

SINGLE 5″ GUN

TWIN 3″ MOUNT   MK 56 DIRECTOR

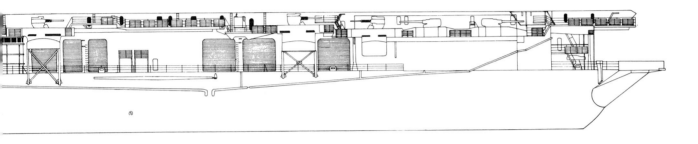

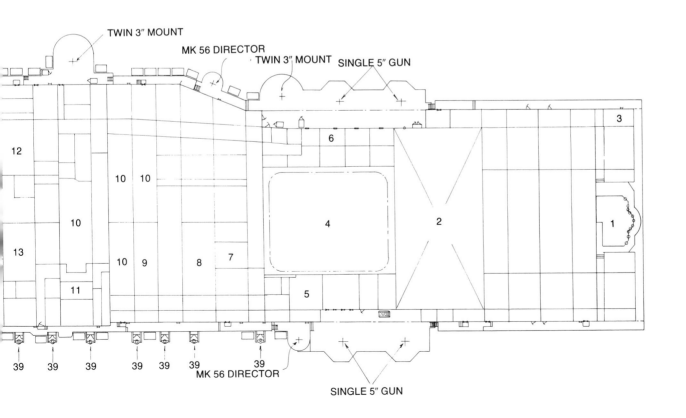

TWIN 3" MOUNT

MK 56 DIRECTOR

TWIN 3" MOUNT

SINGLE 5" GUN

12

10   10

10

13

10   9   8   7

11

6

5

3

4

2

1

39   39   39   39   39   39   39

MK 56 DIRECTOR

SINGLE 5" GUN

USS *Kearsarge*—Bridges and Mast Platforms

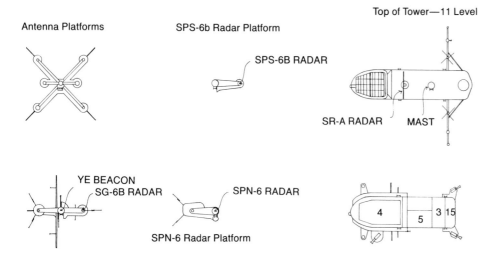

Antenna Platforms

SPS-6b Radar Platform

SPS-6B RADAR

Top of Tower—11 Level

SR-A RADAR   MAST

YE BEACON
SG-6B RADAR   SPN-6 RADAR

SPN-6 Radar Platform

SG-6b Radar and YE Beacon Platforms

Forward Surface Lookout Station—10 Level

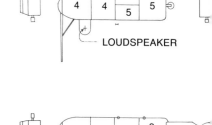

Tower at 09 Level

LOUDSPEAKER

Tower at 08 Level

Key to Bridge Decks
1. Supplementary room
2. Flag message center
3. Radar room
4. Uptake
5. Radio room
6. Tactical flag plot
7. Chief of staff's sea cabin
8. Admiral's sea cabin
9. CCA equipment room
10. Pilothouse
11. Captain's plot and message center
12. Forward AA control station
13. Aerological office
14. Office
15. Forward lookout surface station

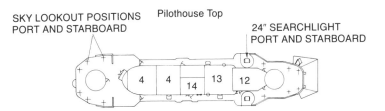

SKY LOOKOUT POSITIONS
PORT AND STARBOARD

Pilothouse Top

24" SEARCHLIGHT
PORT AND STARBOARD

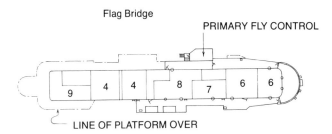

Flag Bridge

PRIMARY FLY CONTROL

LINE OF PLATFORM OVER

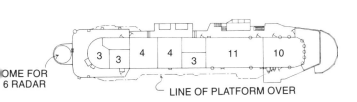

OME FOR
6 RADAR

LINE OF PLATFORM OVER

Navigating Bridge

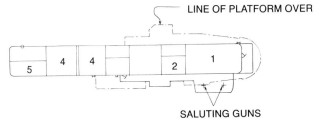

LINE OF PLATFORM OVER

SALUTING GUNS

Communication Platform

General arrangement plans of the *Antietam* as she appeared in 1954. In 1952/53 she was fitted with the prototype angled deck. Later the tripod mast was removed and replaced with a heavier pole mast to carry the newer radars. The funnel uptakes were given sloping caps as shown in the drawing to minimize the effect of smoke on the mast antennas.

USS *Antietam*—Starboard Outboard Profile

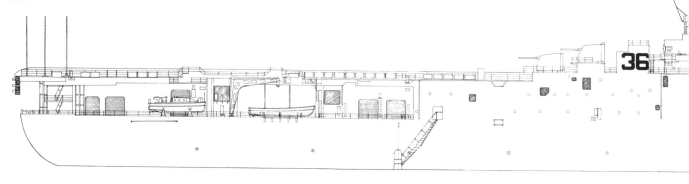

USS *Antietam*—Port Outboard Profile

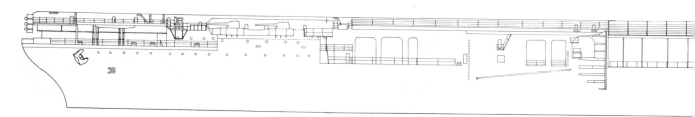

USS *Antietam*—Flight Deck

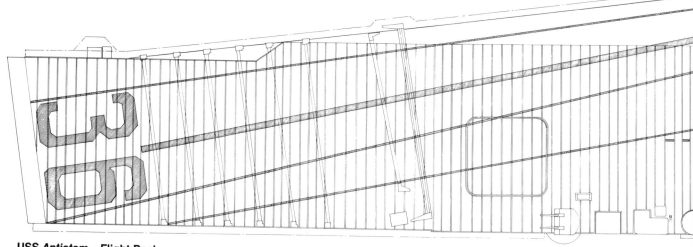

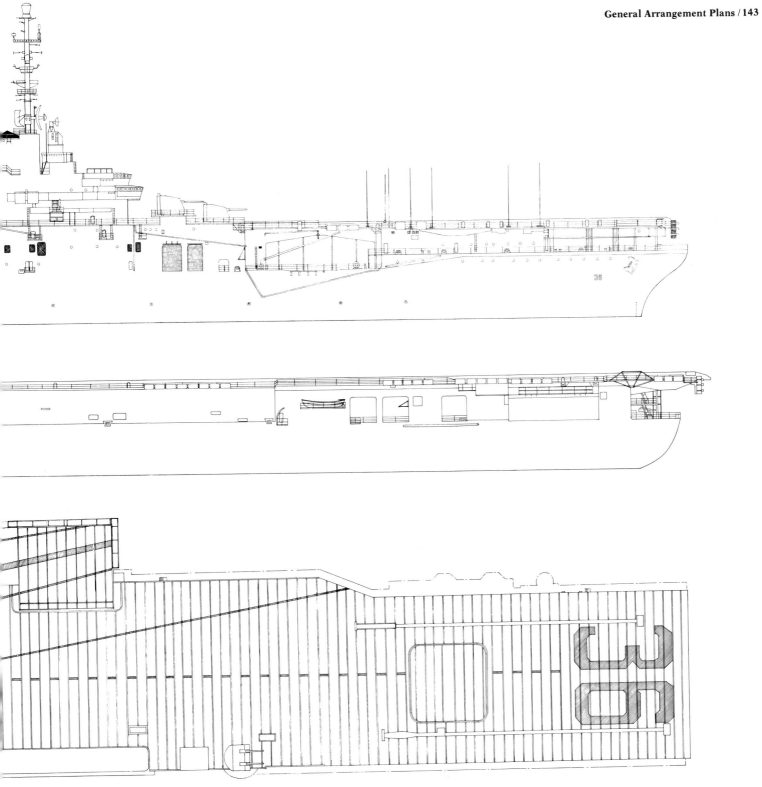

General arrangement plans of the *Intrepid* as she appeared in 1969/70. She was one of those of the class that received the SCB-27c conversion in the early 1950s and subsequent upgrades to keep her fit for front-line service as an attack carrier. The twin 3-inch mounts fitted at the time of conversion were gradually reduced in number until none were left, although she still retains four single 5-inch mounts of prewar design controlled by two Mk 56 directors, one port, one starboard. She has a fully angled deck, C11 steam catapults, two deck-edge elevators, and an enlarged forward centerline elevator. The flight deck has positions marked out for the spotting of helicopters when she operated in the role of an ASW carrier (CVS). Radars carried are SPS-10, SPS-29, SPS-30, SPN-12, SPN-6, and SPN-35, the last in a radome extending from the aft end of the island.

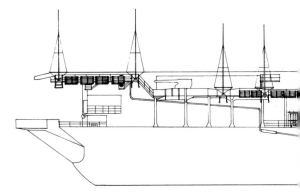

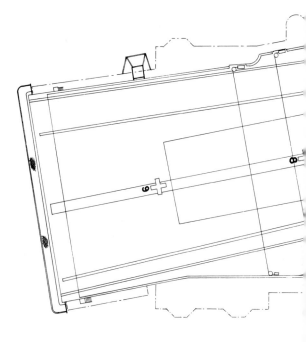

USS *Intrepid*—Flight Deck

USS *Intrepid*—Port Outboard Profile

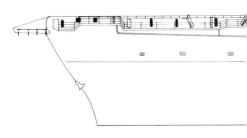

Key to Gallery Deck

1. Secondary conning station
2. Crew's berthing
3. Crew's washroom and WC
4. 5″ handling room
5. Mk 56 director room
6. Gun control room
7. Pyrotechnics stowage
8. Catapult steam receivers
9. Gas station
10. Valve room
11. Catapult equipment
12. Television studio
13. Stores
14. Radio transmitter room
15. Electronics spare parts
16. Fire bomb stowage
17. WCs
18. Junior officers' bunk room
19. Cabins
20. Bomb elevator
21. Bomb elevator machinery room
22. Admiral's stateroom
23. Admiral's bath
24. Admiral's cabin
25. Admiral's pantry
26. Captain's cabin
27. Captain's stateroom
28. Captain's stateroom
29. Confidential book room
30. Captain's pantry
31. Chief of staff's cabin
32. Chief of staff's stateroom
33. Chief of staff's bath
34. CIC
35. Officers' washroom and WC
36. Air conditioning machinery room
37. Antisubmarine Combat Activity Center
38. Flag operations office
39. Radar control room
40. Radar data distribution room
41. Air charts and files
42. Flag office
43. Air department office
44. Flag office
45. Operations department office
46. Radio central (unsecured)
47. Security message processing room
48. Radio central
49. Main communications station
50. Air operations
51. Fan room
52. Radar power supply room
53. Carrier air traffic control central
54. Air intercept
55. Mk 25 radar room
56. Security teletype room
57. Crypto room
58. Electronics material office
59. Electronics office
60. Electronics test equipment issue room
61. Aviation ordnance tool issue room
62. Electronic countermeasures room
63. Squadron locker room
64. Avionics room
65. Sonobuoy storage
66. Avionics spare parts stowage
67. Avionics test equipment room
68. Squadron office
69. Squadron armory
70. Radar nacelles storage
71. 5500-lb bomb elevator
72. Electronic maintenance office
73. Radio transmitter office
74. Audiometric testing room
75. Aircraft ammunition belting room
76. Fire control and optical repair shop
77. Lighting shop
78. Air group locker room
79. Barrier storeroom
80. Mk 56 director control room
81. Legal office
82. Squadron personnel office
83. Maintenance office
84. Arresting gear repair office
85. Crew's shelter
86. Supply radio room
87. Parachute packing room

USS *Intrepid*—Gallery Deck

SINGLE 5″ GUN

SINGLE 5″ GUN

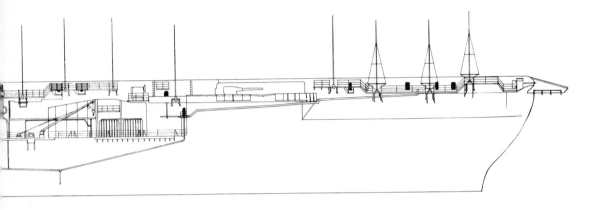

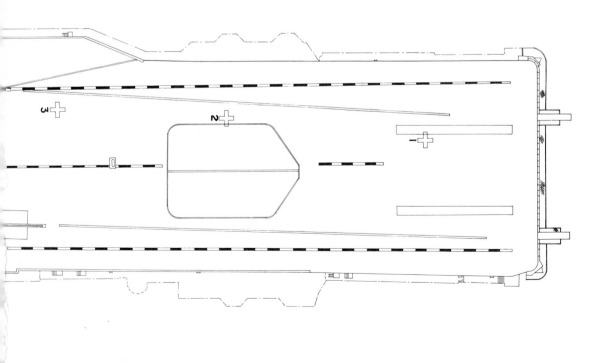

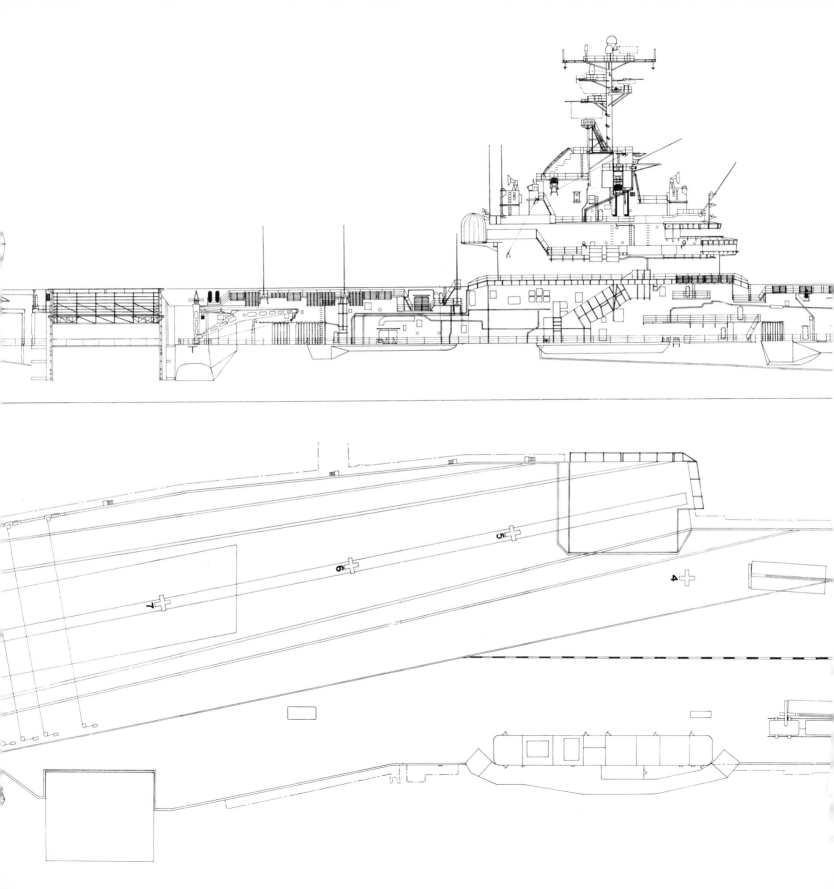

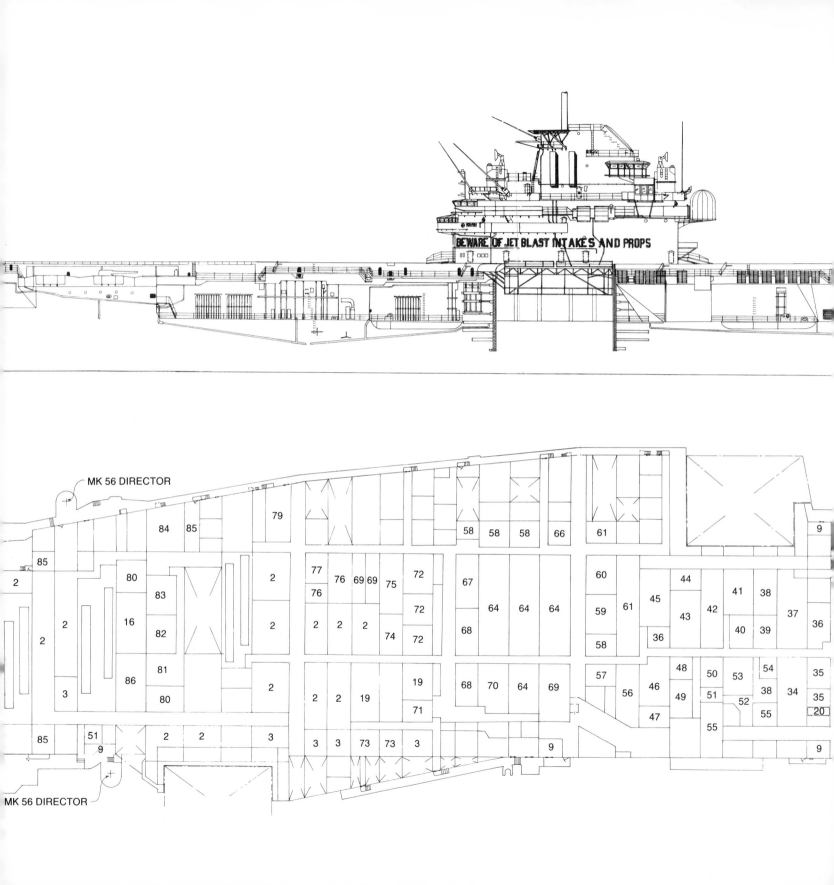

BEWARE OF JET BLAST INTAKES AND PROPS

MK 56 DIRECTOR

MK 56 DIRECTOR

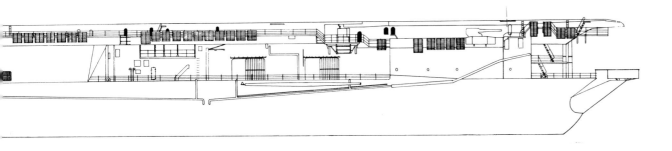

SINGLE 5″ GUN

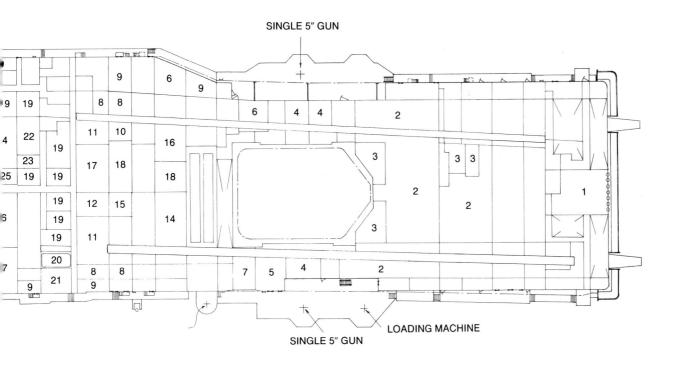

SINGLE 5″ GUN

LOADING MACHINE

Key to Forecastle Deck
1. Junior officers' bunk room
2. Cabins
3. Washroom and WC
4. Elevator trunk
5. Ammunition hoist
6. Catapult steam receivers
7. 16,000-lb bomb elevator
8. Projection room
9. Airborne early-warning radar room
10. Boiler room uptake
11. Uptakes
12. Master at arms
13. 5500-lb bomb elevator
14. Flame-proof sliding hangar door
15. Fire bomb stowage
16. Bomb stowage
17. 26' motor whaleboat
18. Sliding doors
19. Aviation stores office and ready issue room
20. Tool locker room
21. Squadron gear
22. Carpenter's shop
23. CO_2 transfer shop
24. Parachute drying room
25. Paint mixing room
26. Potato locker
27. Vent trunk
28. Bomb elevator

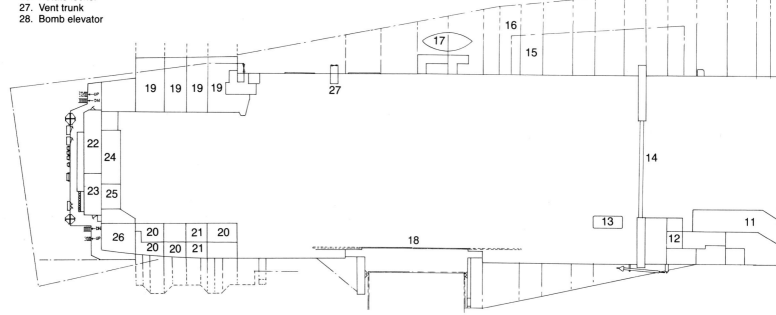

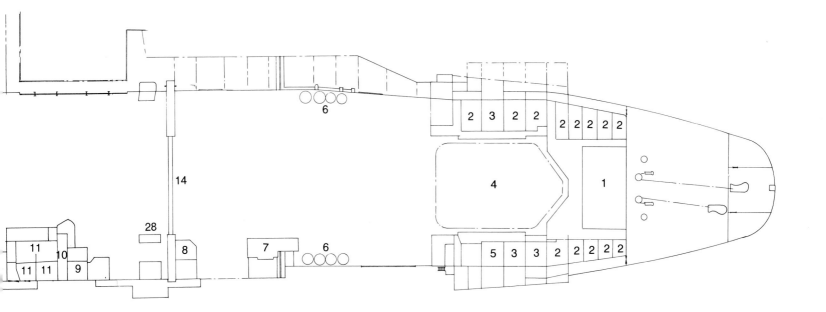

Key to Hangar Deck
1. Cabin
2. Washroom
3. Sonar equipment
4. Elevator opening
5. Catapult steam receivers
6. Bomb elevator
7. Gas station
8. Winch
9. Flame-proof sliding hangar doors
10. Uptakes
11. Storage battery shop
12. Office
13. Photography rooms
14. Hangar deck gear
15. Food stowage
16. Trash burner room
17. Boat shop
18. Sliding doors
19. Fire bomb stowage
20. Fire bomb stowage
21. Wing stowage
22. Tool issue room
23. Ammunition hoist
24. Aviation shop
25. Air frame shop
26. Tool issue room
27. Parachute drying room
28. Shipfitters' shop

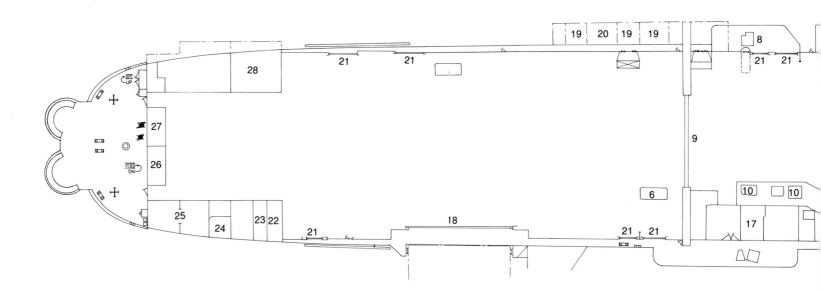

USS *Intrepid*—Hangar Deck

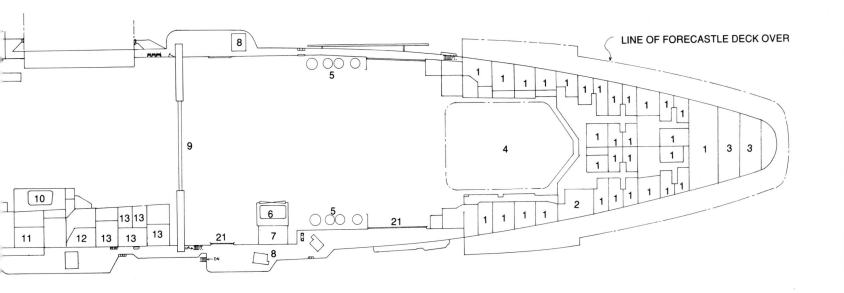

LINE OF FORECASTLE DECK OVER

USS *Intrepid*—Bridges and Mast Platforms

Key to Bridges and Radar Platforms
1. Air conditioning and machinery room
2. SPS-29 radar room
3. Flag message room
4. SPS-30 radar room
5. Uptakes
6. Radio room
7. Tactical flag plot
8. Chief of staff's sea cabin
9. Admiral's sea cabin
10. Sea cabin
11. Radar room
12. Pilothouse
13. Captain's sea cabin
14. Chart house
15. UHF room
16. Aerological room
17. SPN-8 radar
18. Television camera room
19. Radar jamming equipment room
20. Primary fly control station
21. Electronic countermeasures room
22. UHF room
23. Aircraft beacon room

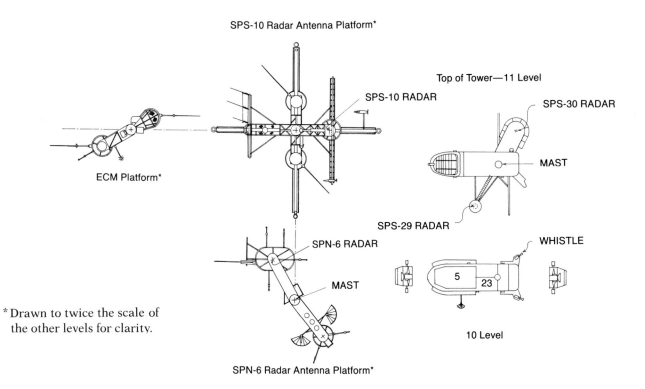

SPS-10 Radar Antenna Platform*

ECM Platform*

SPS-10 RADAR

Top of Tower—11 Level

SPS-30 RADAR

MAST

SPS-29 RADAR

SPN-6 RADAR

MAST

WHISTLE

5   23

SPN-6 Radar Antenna Platform*

10 Level

*Drawn to twice the scale of
the other levels for clarity.

09 Level

Pilothouse Top

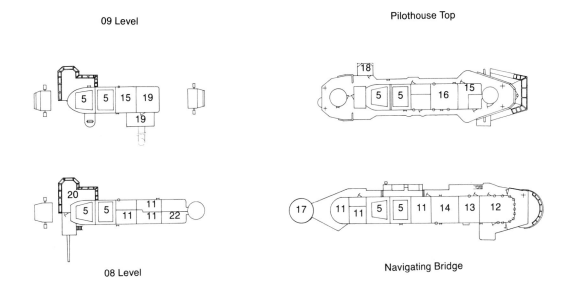

08 Level

Navigating Bridge

Flag Bridge

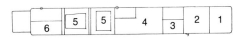

Communication Platform

General arrangement plans of the *Oriskany* as she appeared in 1975, a few months before her withdrawal from service in 1976. The only ship of the class to receive a SCB-125a conversion, the *Oriskany* was probably the most up-to-date of the *Essex* class to serve postwar. Her appearance is very similar to that of the *Intrepid*. Differences include the removal of all guns and retention of type H8 catapults. In radar she is essentially the same as the *Intrepid* with the exception of having the SPS-43a instead of the smaller SPS-29.

USS *Oriskany*—Starboard Outboard Profile

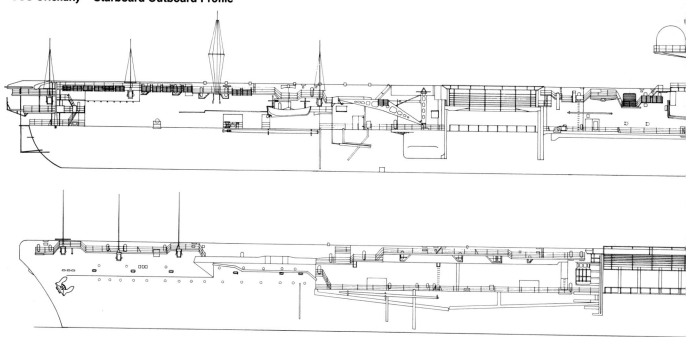

USS *Oriskany*—Port Outboard Profile

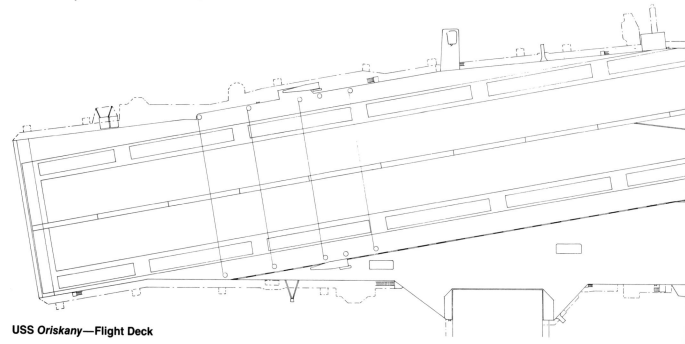

USS *Oriskany*—Flight Deck

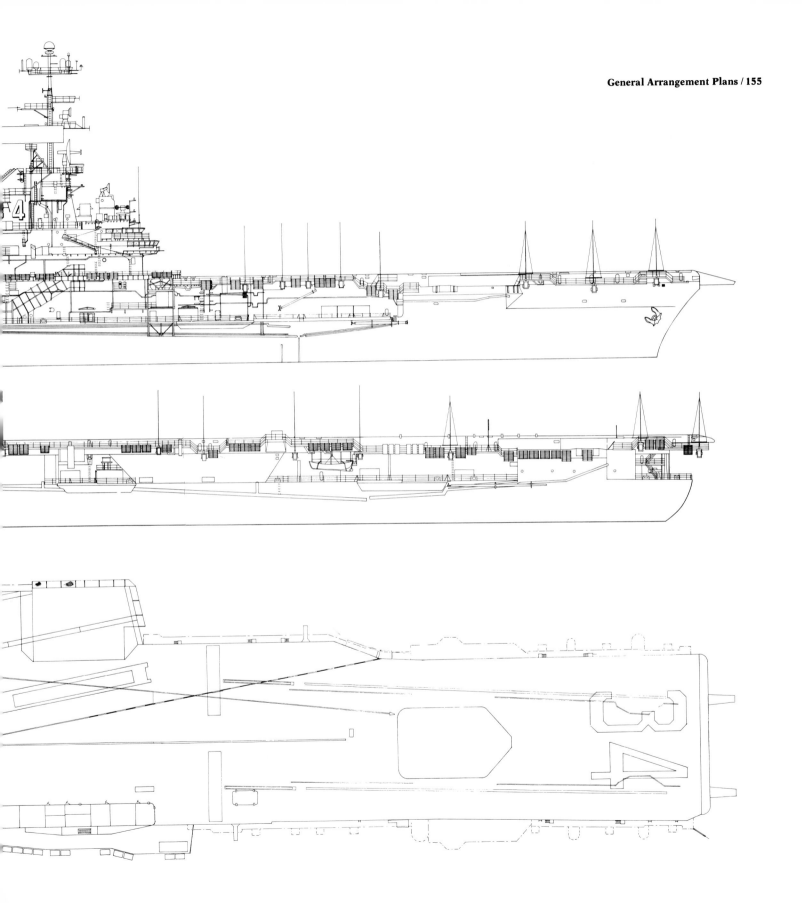

B. General Fittings and Equipment

Towing Tractor, Model T80

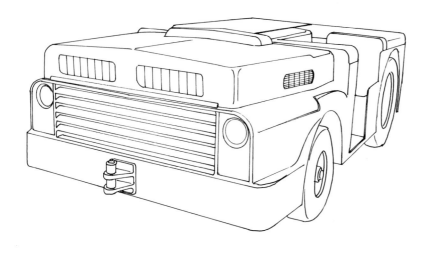

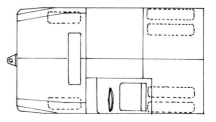

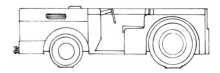

The movement of aircraft around the flight deck was often performed by small tractors. Shown here are types TA-30 and T80, used in the 1950s and 1960s. Despite extensive searches, the author has been unable to locate drawings of tractors for the earlier periods.

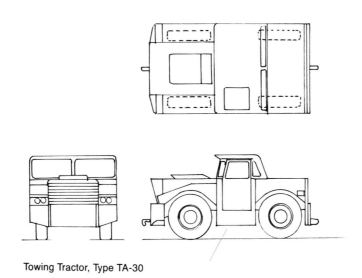

Towing Tractor, Type TA-30

Aircraft Crane

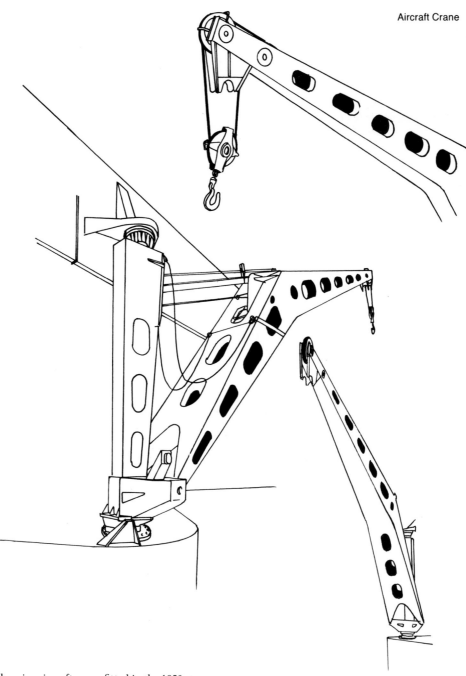

Details of the larger and heavier aircraft crane fitted in the 1950s to handle heavier aircraft.

Mirror Landing Aid

Developed to assist pilots of the faster-landing jets over the slower piston-engine types, the mirror gave the approaching pilot a reflection of his aircraft in relation to the deck landing area. The first American carrier to test this system was the *Bennington* in 1955.

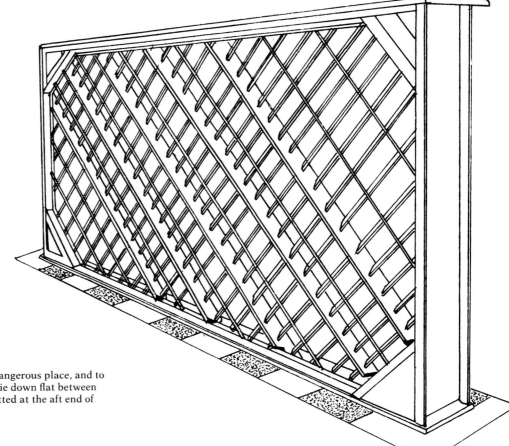

Jet Blast Deflector Shield

The rear end of a jet aircraft about to take off is a dangerous place, and to give a measure of safety a blast shield, one able to lie down flat between launches to allow the positioning of aircraft, was fitted at the aft end of each catapult track.

C. Antennas

Antenna Assembly for Mk 25 Fire Control Radar

An X band radar using a 4-foot parabolic dish antenna fitted on the roof of the Mk 37 directors, the Mk 25 replaced the older Mk 4 and Mk 12/22 radars beginning in the early postwar period.

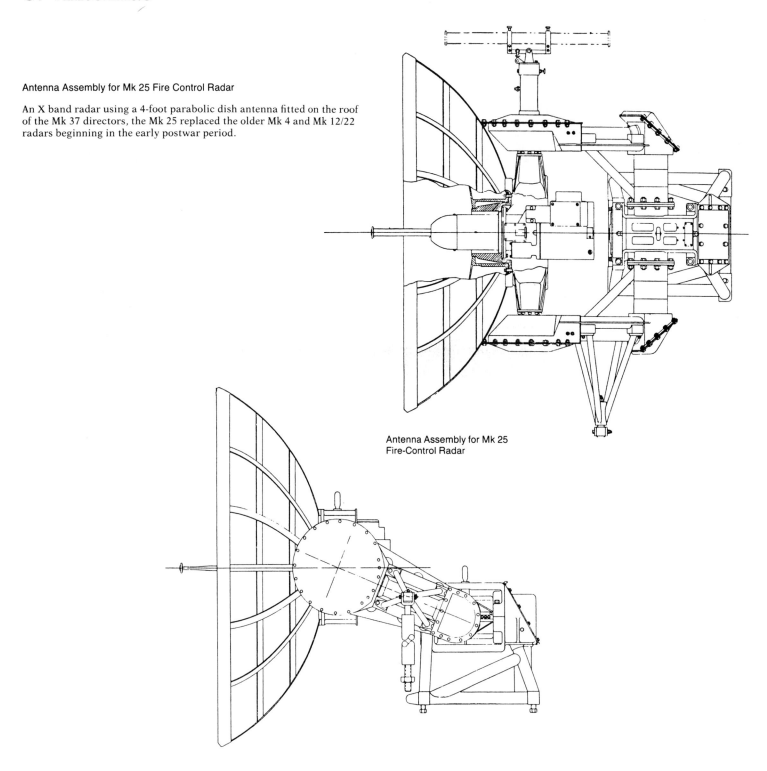

Antenna Assembly for Mk 25
Fire-Control Radar

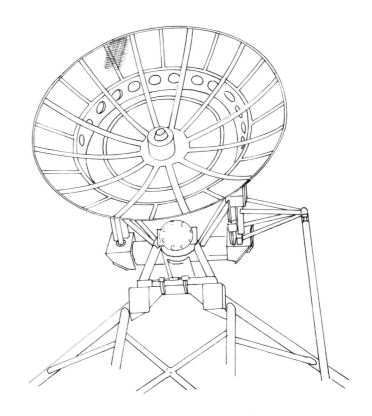

Antenna Assembly for SG-6 Radar

The final production variant of the SG series, it filled the need to provide vertical coverage (zenith search). Two reflectors were used, one for conventional surface search, with the vertical coverage given by a clamshell-style reflector. This was used extensively, with the first installation in the *Essex* in 1946/47.

PLAN VIEW

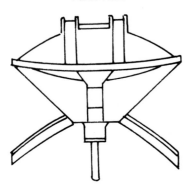

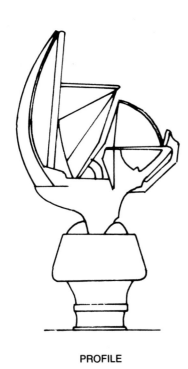

PROFILE

Antenna Assembly for SPS-4 Radar

This antenna was similar to SG-6 but operated in the C band. It was fitted to some of the *Essex* class in the mid-1950s.

PLAN VIEW

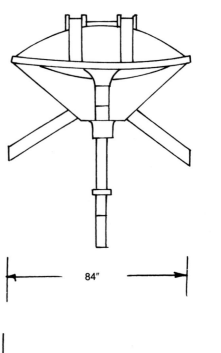

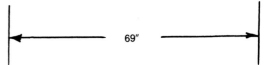

84″

69″

108″

Reflector for zenith search mode

Reflector for surface search mode

Wave guide

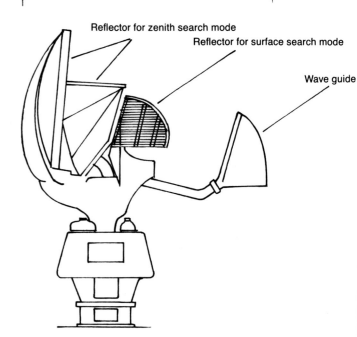

PROFILE

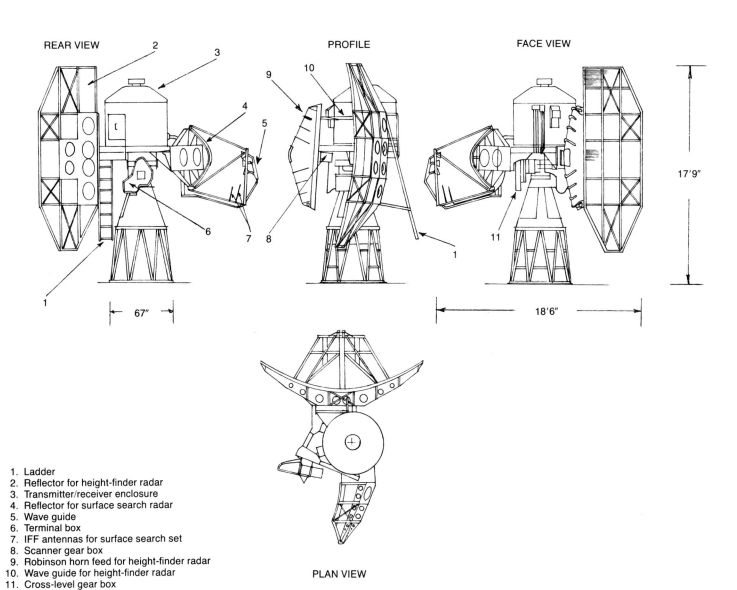

Antenna Assembly for SX Radar

The SX was a combined surface search and height-finder arranged on a single mounting. The *Tarawa* was the first *Essex* to receive an SX, in 1946. The SX was fitted in the late 1940s to all remaining active ships of the class.

REAR VIEW

PROFILE

FACE VIEW

17'9"

67"

18'6"

PLAN VIEW

1. Ladder
2. Reflector for height-finder radar
3. Transmitter/receiver enclosure
4. Reflector for surface search radar
5. Wave guide
6. Terminal box
7. IFF antennas for surface search set
8. Scanner gear box
9. Robinson horn feed for height-finder radar
10. Wave guide for height-finder radar
11. Cross-level gear box

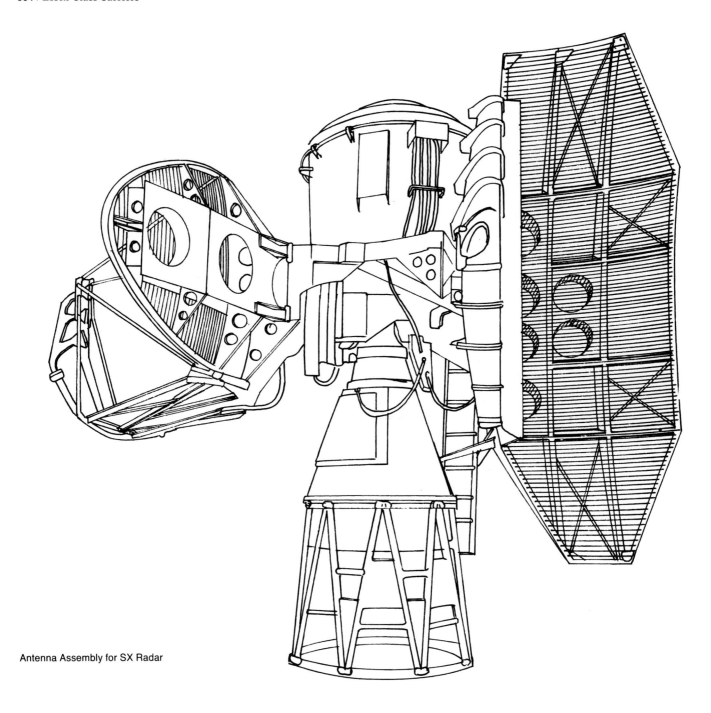

Antenna Assembly for SX Radar

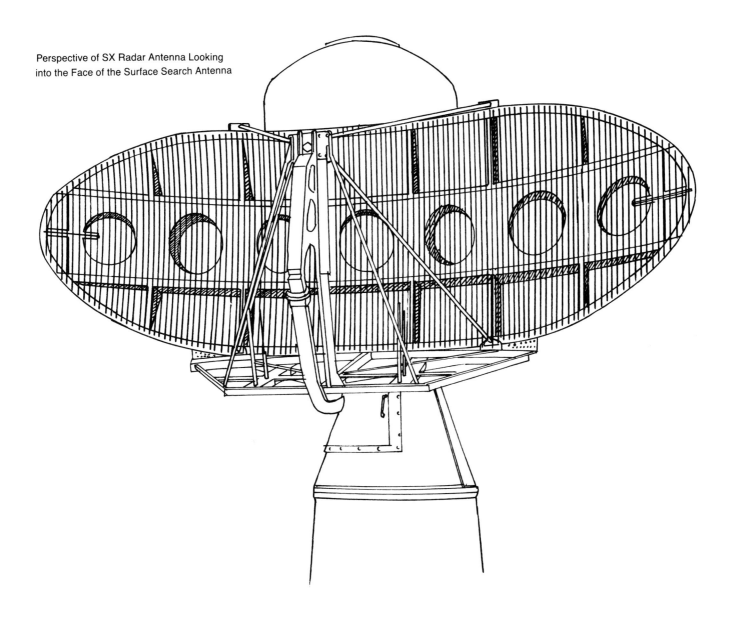

Perspective of SX Radar Antenna Looking
into the Face of the Surface Search Antenna

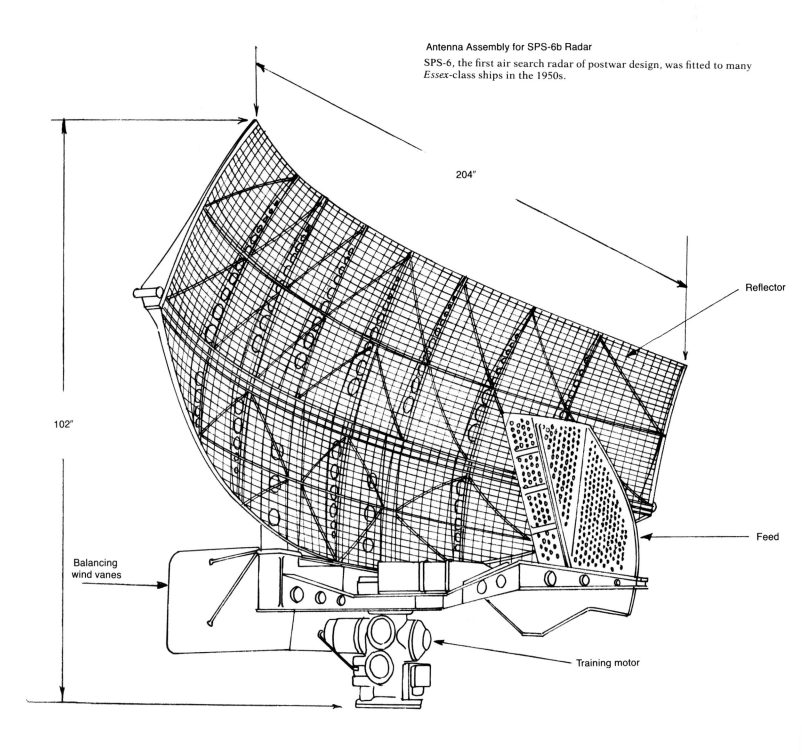

Antenna Assembly for SPS-6b Radar

SPS-6, the first air search radar of postwar design, was fitted to many *Essex*-class ships in the 1950s.

204″

102″

Reflector

Feed

Balancing wind vanes

Training motor

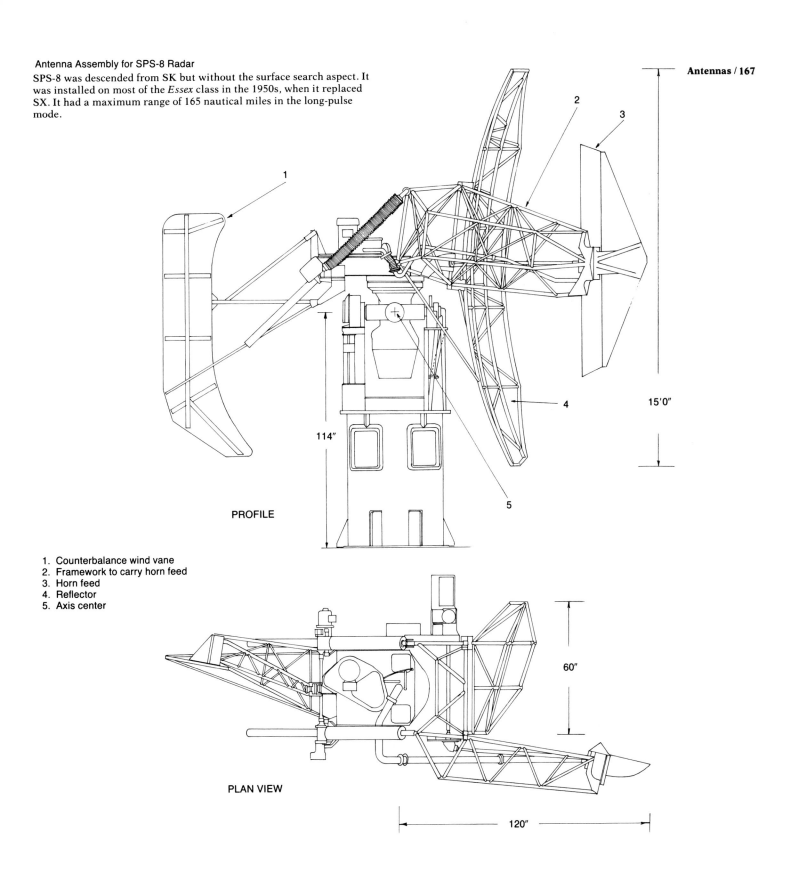

Antenna Assembly for SPS-8 Radar

SPS-8 was descended from SK but without the surface search aspect. It was installed on most of the *Essex* class in the 1950s, when it replaced SX. It had a maximum range of 165 nautical miles in the long-pulse mode.

1
2
3
4
5

15'0"

114"

PROFILE

1. Counterbalance wind vane
2. Framework to carry horn feed
3. Horn feed
4. Reflector
5. Axis center

60"

PLAN VIEW

120"

PROFILE

FACE VIEW

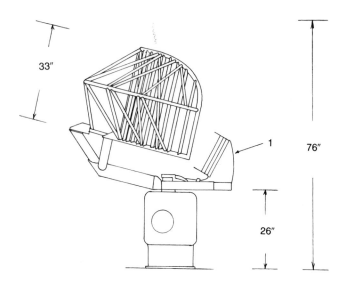

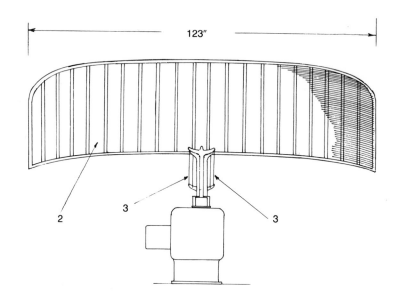

33″

76″

26″

123″

1

2

3

3

Antenna Assembly for SPS-10 Radar

A C band surface search radar, it became the standard set employed after World War II. It employed a 10-foot reflector and had a maximum range of 15 nautical miles.

1. Horn feed
2. Reflector
3. IFF antennas

PLAN VIEW   PROFILE

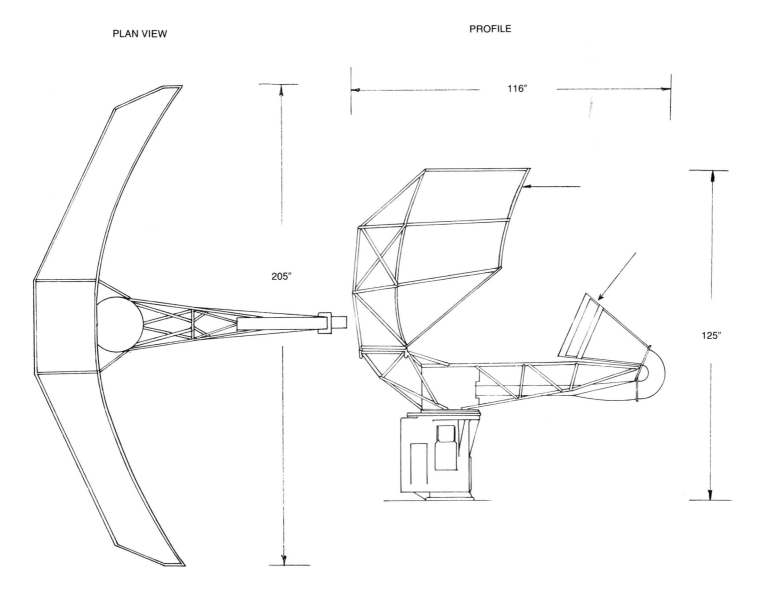

116″

205″

125″

Antenna Assembly for SPS-12 Radar
This was the successor to SPS-6, gradually replacing it during the mid-
to late 1950s.

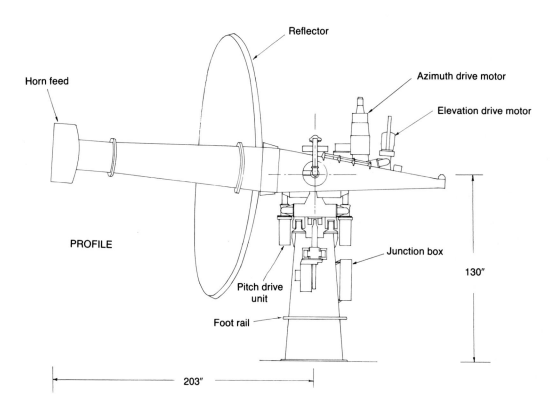

Reflector

Horn feed

Azimuth drive motor

Elevation drive motor

PROFILE

Junction box

130″

Pitch drive
unit

Foot rail

203″

Antenna Assembly for SPS-30 Radar

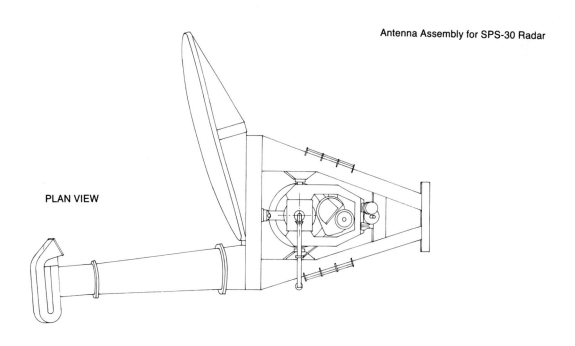

PLAN VIEW

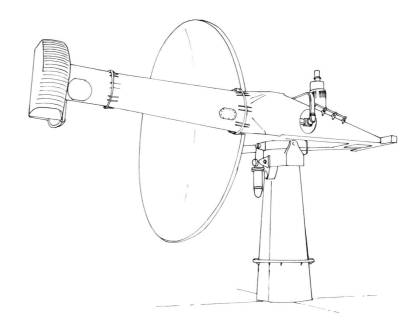

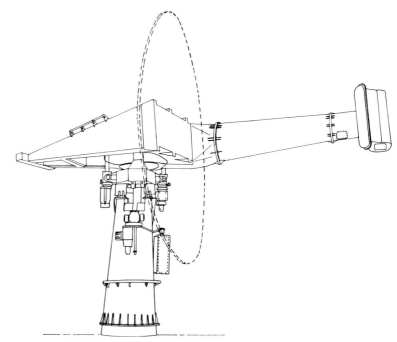

Antenna Assembly for SPS-30 Radar

This pencil-beam height-finder, descended from SX and SPS-8, was able to achieve a 240-nautical-mile range. The parabolic reflector is 15 feet by 12 feet. The set was first delivered to fleet units in May 1962 and installed on many of the *Essex* class.

PLAN VIEW

ANTENNA FACE SHOWING REFLECTING DIPOLES AND MOUNTING

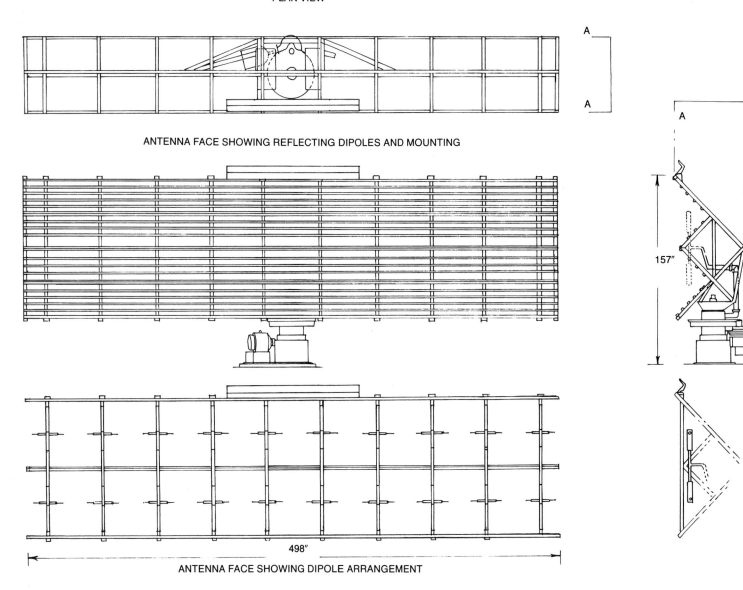

498"

ANTENNA FACE SHOWING DIPOLE ARRANGEMENT

Antenna Assembly for SPS-43a Radar

The *Oriskany* was one of only a few ships of the class to be fitted with a
set of this very long range (300 nautical miles) air search outfit operating
in the P band.

PLAN VIEW

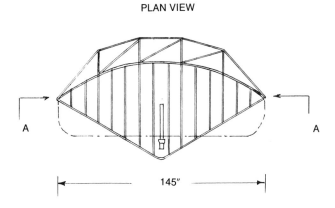

145″

Antenna Assembly for SPN-6 Radar

This carrier-controlled approach (CCA) radar was introduced in the early 1950s and fitted in all converted *Essex*-class vessels.

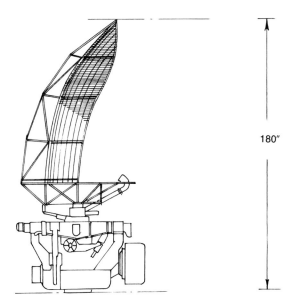

180″

PROFILE

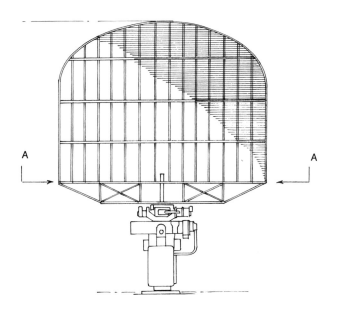

FACE VIEW

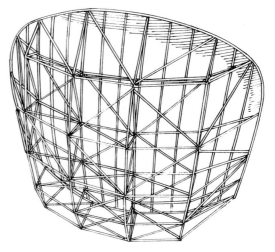

REAR PERSPECTIVE

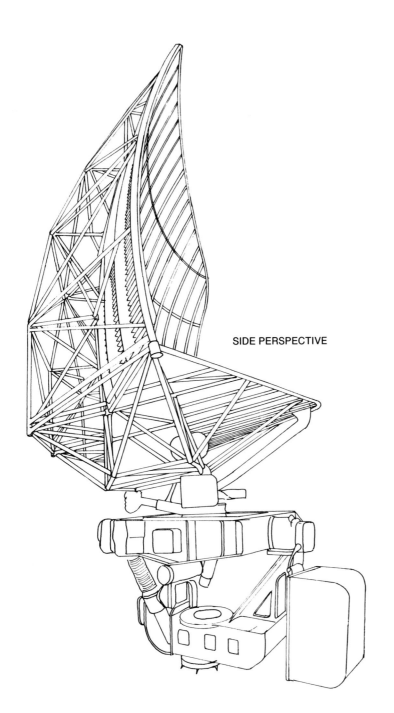

SIDE PERSPECTIVE

Antenna Assembly for SPN-6 Radar

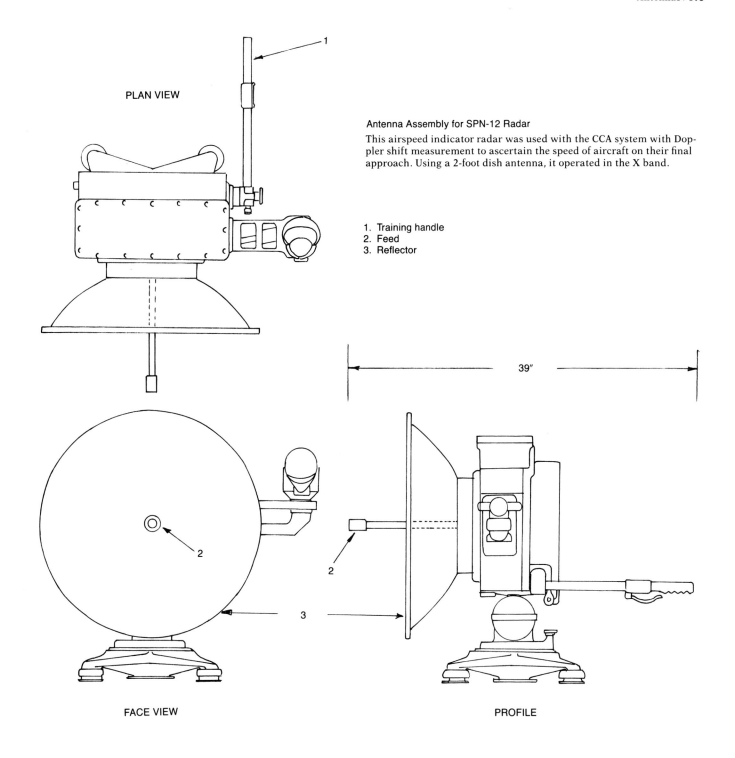

PLAN VIEW

Antenna Assembly for SPN-12 Radar

This airspeed indicator radar was used with the CCA system with Doppler shift measurement to ascertain the speed of aircraft on their final approach. Using a 2-foot dish antenna, it operated in the X band.

1. Training handle
2. Feed
3. Reflector

39″

FACE VIEW

PROFILE

Antenna Assembly for SPN-43 Radar

A replacement for SPN-6 radar, it came into service in the late 1960s and was fitted to the *Oriskany* only.

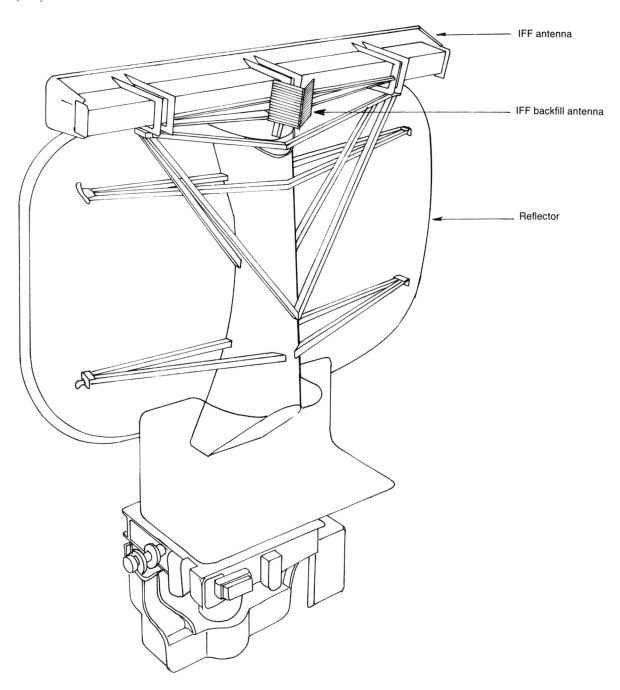

IFF antenna

IFF backfill antenna

Reflector

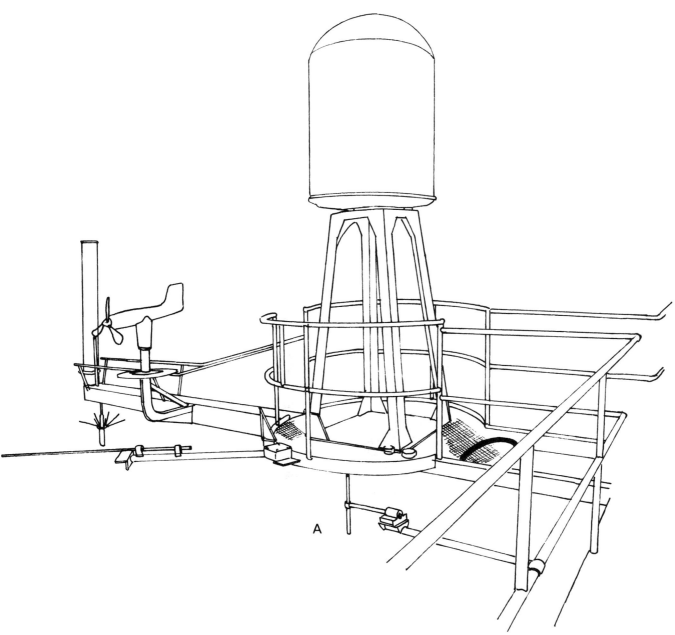

Perspective Views (A, B, C, D, E) of the *Intrepid*'s Various Antenna
Platforms and Equipment Fitted Thereon, Circa 1970

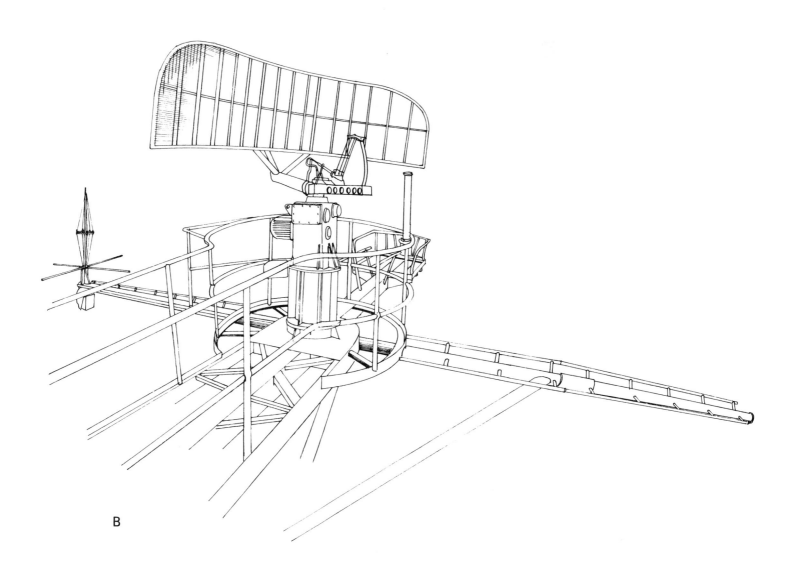

B

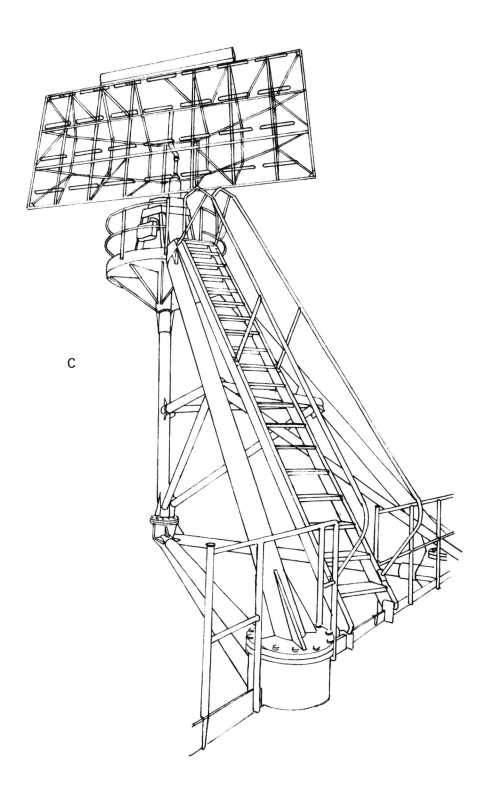

C

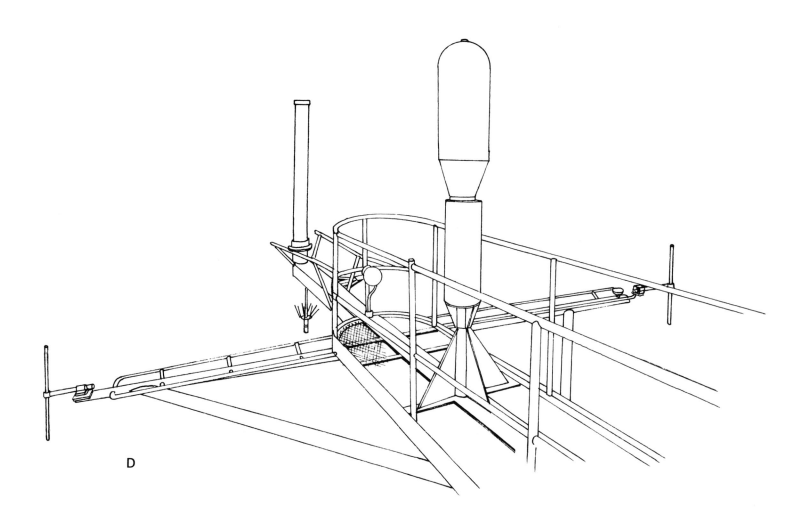

D

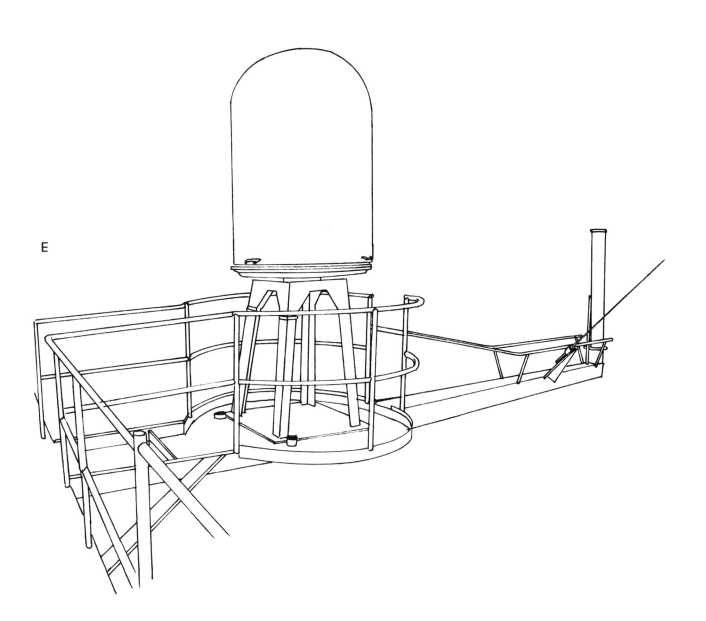

E

D. Miscellaneous

1. Nonskid paint over steel
2. ⅛" overlay
3. ¼" overlay
4. ½" overlay
5. ¼" overlay plus aluminum
6. Panels
7. 25-lb special treatment steel
8. Panels with added polyurethane totaling ¾"

PANELS = Prefabricated 5/32" polyurethane-clad hickory plywood panels plus nonskid paint.

OVERLAY = Thickness of polyurethane laid over planking plus nonskid paint.

Deck Covering Arrangements for SCB-27c Conversions

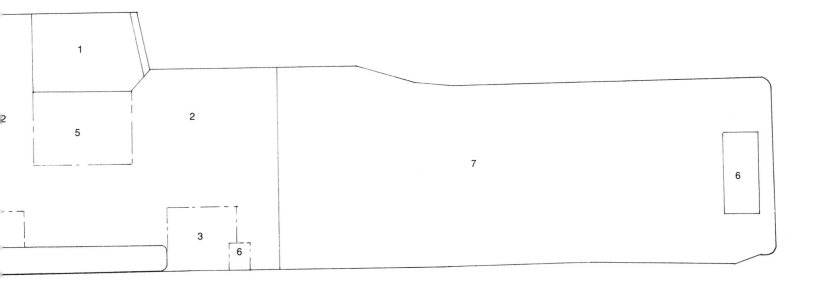

Flight Deck Markings (circa 1969)

Because of the ability of carriers fitted with an angled deck to land and launch planes simultaneously, the movement of planes on the flight deck became more complicated, and this is reflected in the increase in deck markings. The most noticeable innovation is the perimeter guidelines for the landing-on area: without a safety barrier between it and the forward area where planes would be spotted, a wrong angle of approach and landing could have serious consqeuences. Other additions are the various line-up and launch lines on the fore part of the deck.

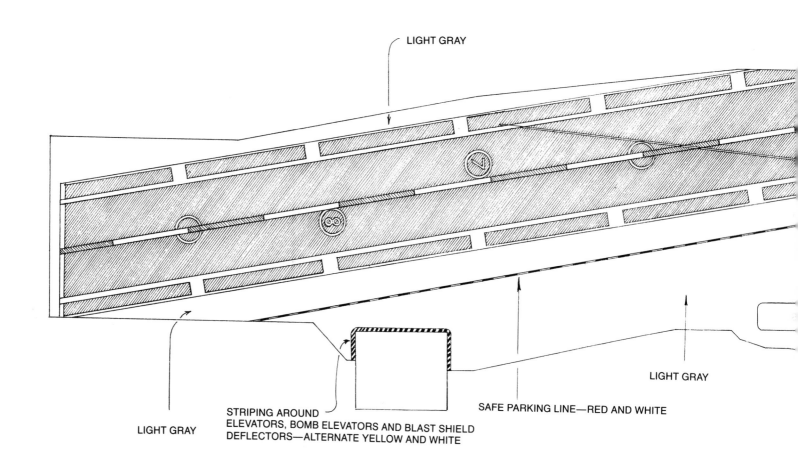

LIGHT GRAY

LIGHT GRAY

LIGHT GRAY

STRIPING AROUND ELEVATORS, BOMB ELEVATORS AND BLAST SHIELD DEFLECTORS—ALTERNATE YELLOW AND WHITE

SAFE PARKING LINE—RED AND WHITE

Color Notes
Flight Deck Light gray
Launch lines White
Line-up lines White
Ship identification number
at bow White

Helicopter Positions
Circles (outline) White
Circles (inner) Dark gray
Numerals White

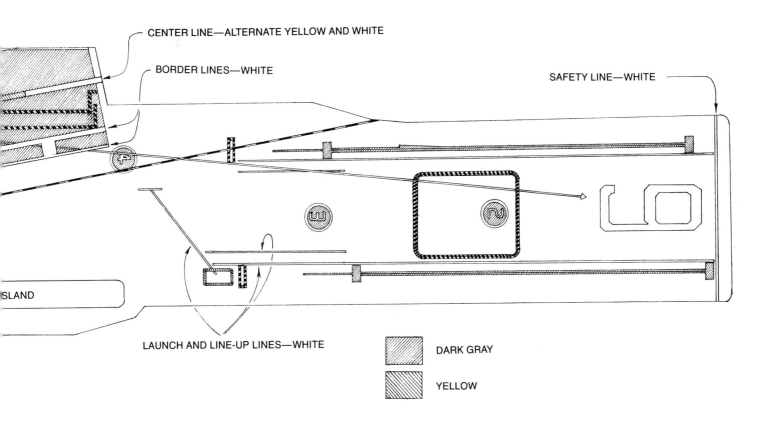

CENTER LINE—ALTERNATE YELLOW AND WHITE

BORDER LINES—WHITE

SAFETY LINE—WHITE

ISLAND

LAUNCH AND LINE-UP LINES—WHITE

DARK GRAY

YELLOW

Characteristics

After the secretary of the navy had approved a new ship or class of ship, the major features of the design were described by the General Board, and through the chief of naval operations were distributed to the Bureaus of Construction and Repair, Engineering, Ordnance, Aeronautics, and Navigation. To enable the reader to see exactly how an approved new ship design was described within the navy, the characteristics for the Essex design (CV9-F) are given below.

31 January, 1940.

G.B. No.420-5
(Serial No. 1861)

From: Chairman General Board;
To   :   Secretary of the Navy.

SUBJECT: Aircraft Carrier CV-9—Characteristics.
ENCLOSURE: (A) Characteristics for CV-9.

1. The General Board has made exhaustive studies of the most advantageous characteristics to be included in aircraft carriers without the former restriction of displacement as a limiting factor. The enclosure contains the characteristics the Board recommends as being essential for the maximum practicable effectiveness of this type of ship.

2. The displacement of the aircraft carrier recommended by the Board for construction as CV-9 has increased from the standard displacement of 20,000 tons of the *Yorktown* class to approximately 26,500 tons. This increase in standard displacement chiefly is due to the following items:

(a) An increase in length of flight deck to permit effective operation of 4 squadrons of aircraft in one launching operation;

(b) Greatly increased subdivision, including installation of power plant in a larger number of smaller compartments and a rearrangement of these compartments so that no one hit can put out of commission the entire power plant; a triple bottom that greatly increases resistance to damage from mines; an arrangement of side compartments that gives excellent protection against torpedo hits.

(c) An increase in aircraft gasoline capacity by one-fourth, thus permitting more extensive aircraft operations.

(d) An increase in armament from 8 to 12 five-inch double purpose guns.

(e) An increase in protection against bombs and projectiles, and against splinters and machine gun bullets for exposed personnel. The greatest increase has been the inclusion of an armored main deck designed to resist 1,000-lb. bombs.

(f) An essential increase in propulsive power from 120,000 to 150,000 S.H.P.

3. The General Board is strongly of the opinion that the advantages to be gained by the increase in standard displacement far outweigh the additional cost involved and feels confident that the resulting ship will be a very great improvement over the *Yorktown* class.

W. R. Sexton

30 January, 1940

AIRCRAFT CARRIER CV-9 CHARACTERISTICS

1. *Aircraft Capacity:*

(a) *Complement:* Designed for effective operation of one group of aircraft, comprising four (4) squadrons, in one launching operation from flight deck; a total of 74 aircraft, consisting of 18 VF, 38 VSB and 18 VT types.

(b) *Spares:* Capable of stowing 50 percent of complement of aircraft, as spares, disassembled.

(c) *Additional:* Capable of accommodating one additional operating squadron consisting of 18 VF and 1 VSB.

2. *Hull:*

(a) *Standard Displacement:* Minimum compatible with inclusion of all essential characteristics; approximating 26,500 tons.

(b) *Beam:* Not to exceed limit for passage of present locks of Panama Canal.

(c) *Type:* 'Offset Island' type, with fixed smoke stacks.

(d) *Island Structure:* As small as practicable for inclusion of all essential activities; stream-lined.

(e) *Flight Deck:* Maximum practicable width, but not less than 80 feet throughout.

Maximum practicable length, but not less than 850 feet over all.

(f) *Hangar:* Open sided, capable of complete closure, well ventilated to permit warming up aircraft engines when closed.

Maximum practicable length and width compatible with structural and other requirements.

Minimum clear height throughout of 18 feet below overhead girders.

Heating arrangements for maintaining temperature of 40° Fahr. when outside temperature is zero.

(g) *Subdivision:* Most complete practicable, including four firerooms in pairs and two engine rooms, with one engine room between two pairs of firerooms, and with maximum practicable number of intact torpedo bulkheads.

Triple bottom under machinery spaces and equivalent bottom protection under magazines.

Magazines, main power plant units, steering gear, fuel oil and gasoline tanks located and arranged to obtain maximum practicable protection against projectiles, torpedoes, bombs and mines.

Magazine flats of maximum thickness compatible with weight and other primary considerations.

(h) *Seaworthiness:* Best practicable aircraft platform with excellent maneuvering ability, and capable of maintaining high speed under rough sea conditions. Inherent transverse stability under all conditions of loading.

(i) *Ship Control:* Located in Island Structure, with adequate space for all essential activities, and with as complete all around and overhead vision as practicable.

Fitted with all necessary appliances of latest approved designs.

A Secondary Ship Control Station located in most advantageous position available, without interfering with other essential features of ship.

(j) *Damage Control:* Fitted with latest approved facilities for control of damage.

(k) *Gas Protection:* In accordance with latest approved policy.

(l) *Accommodations:* Fitted as flagship, and with quarters, berthing and office spaces for approved complement of ship and staff, and of five aircraft squadrons.

Complete cafeteria system for messing ship and squadron enlisted personnel.

3. *Aviation Features*:

(a) *Elevators:* Three of express type; one near each end of hangar with flight deck openings so located as to serve most advantageous operation of aircraft; one with flight deck opening between bow and stern arresting gears and as close to island structure as practicable; all capable of accommodating one modern VT type aircraft with wings folded.

(b) *Catapults:* Three of flush deck type; two forward on flight deck capable of launching VT type of aircraft; and one double action type in hangar capable of launching VSB type of aircraft when fully loaded.

(c) *Air Control:* Located in island structure, with as complete vision of flight deck operations as possible, with ready access to Air Plot and Ship Control.

(d) *Air Plot:* Located in island structure; adequate for operation of five squadrons of aircraft; and equipped with all necessary appliances of latest approved designs.

(e) *Flag Plot:* Located in island structure; of adequate size, equipped with all essential appliances of latest approved designs; readily accessible to Flag Radio.

To have as complete vision as practicable without interference with essential vision of Ship Control and Air Control.

(f) *Ready Rooms:* Located so as to permit ready access to flight deck, with one ready room for each of four aircraft squadrons, at least.

Effectively air conditioned and otherwise equipped for comfort of personnel.

(g) *Gasoline Capacity:* At least 220,000 gallons. Gasoline supply system capable of supply rate of 1,000 gallons per minute to flight deck and hangar outlets.

(h) *Aircraft Engine Lubricating Oil Capacity:* At least 20,000 gallons.

(i) *Fire Protection:* Special consideration to be given to protection of aircraft, flight deck and hangar space against fire hazard.

(j) *Bomb Stowage:* Adequate for 148–1,000 lb., 450–500 lb. and 522–100 lb. bombs, with additional magazine space for 100 percent increase.

Adequate facilities for rapid supply of bombs to flight deck.

(k) *Torpedo Stowage:* Below deck stowage for 36 Mark XIII, or Mark VII-a, torpedoes, with magazine space for 36 warheads.

Adequate facilities for supplying torpedoes to aircraft on flight deck.

(l) *Ammunition:* Magazine space for standard allowance of aircraft machine gun ammunition and pyrotechnics for five aircraft squadrons.

(m) **Combat Information Center and fighter director station: Located in protected position below fourth deck armor, of adequate size, equipped with all necessary appliances of latest approved designs.*

4. *Armament*:

(a) *Main Battery:* Twelve 5-inch 38-caliber double purpose guns; eight in twin mounts on flight deck, four forward and four aft of island structure; four in single mounts on port galleries extended and stepped down from flight deck, two forward and two aft, with maximum practicable area of overhead fire.

(b) *Secondary Battery:* **Forty-four** [At least twenty-four] **40 mm** [1.1-inch] A.A. machine guns in quadruple mounts; four mounts on island structure; **three** [two] mounts on port galleries, **2 mounts at bow, 2 mounts at stern** [one forward and one aft]; **all** so located as to give the clearest possible all around overhead fire.

The [To have installed] largest number of **20 mm** [.50-caliber] A.A. machine guns that can be **mounted and advantageously employed** [accommodated on island structure without interference with other essential features of ship and battery].

*Material in boldface type was added in 1944. Material in brackets was deleted in 1944.

(c) *Ammunition:* 6,200 rounds of 5-inch, with additional space for 20 percent increase; and **about 89,000** [at least 57,000] rounds of **40 mm** [1.1-inch] ammunition **including R.S. ammunition**.

Standard allowance of **20 mm** [.50-caliber] A.A. machine gun and small arms ammunition.

(d) *Fire Control:* **Three** [Two] 5-inch directors, standard remote control.

Standard 40 mm directors. [Six 1.1-inch target directors, with remote control.]

Equipped with [Captain's] target designation system.

(e) *Battle Lookouts:* Two Surface Lookout Stations, one forward and one aft, so located and constructed as to give as complete all around combined vision as practicable; 8 sectors forward and 4 sectors aft.

One Sky Lookout Station so located and constructed as to give as complete all around overhead vision as practicable; as near to Sky Control as practicable; 6 sectors equally spaced.

Adequately equipped for prompt and accurate information.

(f) *Searchlights:* Four 36-inch high powered, fitted for high angle searching, with positive distant control.

5. *Protection:*

(a) *Armor:* Magazines, boiler rooms, engine rooms, steering gear, gasoline tanks, and other vital spaces to be protected by a fourth deck of 60-lb. S.T.S. and by side armor equivalent to 4.5-inch ballistic thickness; transverse bulkheads four inches. This protection should give immunity against 6", 105-lb. A.P. projectiles with 2800 foot-seconds velocity between 11,250 yards (at 90° target angle) and about 18,700 yards.

Main deck approximately 2½ inches total thickness of S.T.S. over same length as protected by protective fourth deck.

No armored conning tower; but pilot house protected by S.T.S. plating, 60 lb. on top, 40 lb. on sides, and 40 lb. or equivalent on bottom.

Directors, director tubes, air control, air plot, flag plot, radio stations, battle lookout stations, and similar locations at least 30 lb. S.T.S. protection against .50 caliber bullets and bomb fragments.

Twin gun mounts and handling rooms at least 50 lb. S.T.S. protection.

Bomb elevators and ammunition hoists at least 40 lb. S.T.S. protection to highest levels practicable.

(b) *Splinter Protection:* Provided for exposed flight and battery personnel wherever feasible without sacrifice in major characteristics.

6. *Propulsion and Power:*

(a) *Speed Ahead:* At least 33 knots at trial displacement equal to full load displacement less one-third fuel and reserve feed water.

(b) *Speed Astern:* Capable of at least 20 knots astern for a period of one hour.

(c) *Endurance:* 20,000 miles at 15 knots, 4 months out of dock.

(d) *Lubricating Oil:* Capacity for twice the amount required for endurance at all speeds.

(d) *Power Plant:* Geared turbine type, operating under tested and approved temperatures and pressures, so designed as to be reliable for speeds ahead and astern as designated. Approximately 150,000 S.H.P.

Arranged as to permit flexible and reliable operation under 50 percent damage to power plant, while giving maximum practicable accessibility for maintenance and overhaul of machinery and for preservation of ship's structure.

(f) *Electric Power:* Four main turbo generators separated as far as practicable and of such capacity that two can carry the battle load.

Auxiliary Diesel power of at least 500 K.W. in two units at suitable locations, capable of limited battery operation.

(g) *Distilling Plant:* Ample for all conditions of operation.

(h) *Potable Water:* Storage capacity for 150,000 gallons potable drinking water.

7. *Communications:*

(a) *Radio:* To meet requirements of Fleet Communication Plans, and to have latest devices for control and detection of aircraft.

(b) *Visual:* Standard day and night equipment, including standard carrier equipment of searchlights for signalling and aircraft operations.

(c) *Sound:* Echo sounding equipment, deep, for navigational purposes.

8. *Miscellaneous:*

(a) *Shops:* Adequate in number and equipment for maintenance and upkeep of ship and for operational repairs and tests for aircraft; combined wherever practicable.

(b) *Fueling:* Equipped for fueling at sea from oil and gasoline tankers, and for re-fueling destroyers.

(c) *Towing:* Fitted for emergency towing only.

(d) *Boats:* Equipped with
Four 50-foot motor launches,
One 36-foot motor launch,
Two 50-foot motor boats, this is 50-foot ML converted,
Three 40-foot motor boats,
One 40-foot motor barge,
Two 26-foot motor whaleboats.

9. *Provisions and Stores:*

(a) G.S.K. Stores, 6 weeks; space for 16 weeks;

(b) Dry Provisions, 6 weeks; space for 16 weeks;

(c) Cold Storage, 3 weeks; space for 6 weeks;

(d) Clothing and Small Stores, 6 weeks; space for 12 weeks;

(e) Ships Store Stock, 6 weeks; space for 16 weeks.

List of Ships

Name/Builder	Laid Down	Commissioned
9 Essex/NN	28 Apr 41	31 Dec 42
10 Yorktown/NN	1 Dec 41	15 Apr 43
11 Intrepid/NN	1 Dec 41	16 Aug 43
12 Hornet/NN	3 Aug 42	29 Nov 43
13 Franklin/NN	7 Dec 42	31 Jan 44
14 Ticonderoga*/NN	1 Feb 43	8 May 44
15 Randolph*/NN	10 May 43	9 Oct 44
16 Lexington/BETHQ	15 July 41	17 Mar 43
17 Bunker Hill/BETHQ	15 Sep 41	24 May 43
18 Wasp/BETHQ	18 Mar 42	24 Nov 43
19 Hancock*/BETHQ	26 Jan 43	15 Apr 44
20 Bennington/NYNY	15 Dec 42	6 Aug 44
21 Boxer*/NN	13 Sep 43	16 Apr 45
31 Bon Homme Richard/NYNY	1 Feb 43	26 Nov 44
32 Leyte*/NN	21 Feb 44	11 Apr 46
33 Kearsarge*/NYNY	1 Mar 44	2 Mar 46
34 Oriskany*/NYNY	1 May 44	25 Sep 50
35 Reprisal*/NYNY	1 Jul 44	Not completed
36 Antietam*/PHNY	14 Mar 43	28 Jun 45
37 Princeton*/PHNY	14 Sep 43	18 Nov 45
38 Shangri-La*/NORNY	15 Jan 43	15 Sep 44
39 Lake Champlain*/NORNY	15 Mar 43	3 Jun 45
40 Tarawa*/NORNY	5 Jan 44	8 Dec 45
45 Valley Forge*/PHNY	7 Sep 44	3 Nov 46
46 Iwo Jima*/NN	29 Jan 45	Not completed
47 Philippine Sea*/BETHQ	19 Aug 44	11 May 46

*Long-hull ship.

The Naval Institute Press is the book-publishing arm of the U.S. Naval Institute, a private, nonprofit professional society for members of the sea services and civilians who share an interest in naval and maritime affairs. Established in 1873 at the U.S. Naval Academy in Annapolis, Maryland, where its offices remain today, the Naval Institute has more than 100,000 members worldwide.

Members of the Naval Institute receive the influential monthly naval magazine *Proceedings* and substantial discounts on fine nautical prints, ship and aircraft photos, and subscriptions to the Institute's recently inaugurated quarterly, *Naval History.* They also have access to the transcripts of the Institute's Oral History Program and may attend any of the Institute-sponsored seminars regularly offered around the country.

The book-publishing program, begun in 1898 with basic guides to naval practices, has broadened its scope in recent years to include books of more general interest. Now the Naval Institute Press publishes more than forty new titles each year, ranging from how-to books on boating and navigation to battle histories, biographies, ship guides, and novels. Institute members receive discounts on the Press's more than 300 books.

For a free catalog describing books currently available and for further information about U.S. Naval Institute membership, please write to:

Membership Department
U.S. Naval Institute
Annapolis, Maryland 21402

or call, toll-free, 800-233-USNI.